KAKAMORA

Dr. Charles Fox, M.B.E.

KAKAMORA

by

Charles E. Fox
M.B.E., M.A., D.Litt.

London
HODDER & STOUGHTON

Copyright © 1962 by Charles E. Fox.

First printed 1962

MADE AND PRINTED IN GREAT BRITAIN FOR
HODDER AND STOUGHTON LIMITED, LONDON
BY C. TINLING AND CO. LIMITED, LIVERPOOL,
LONDON AND PRESCOT

CONTENTS

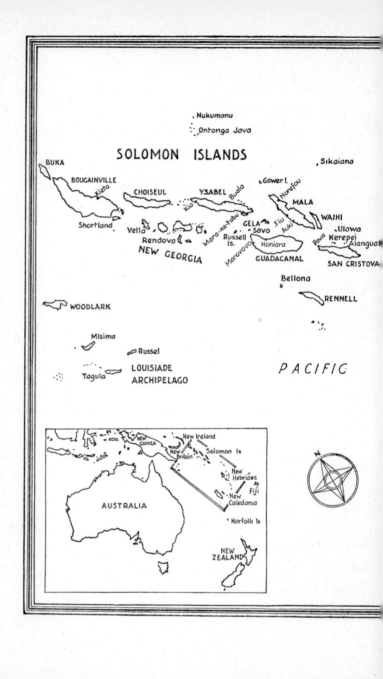

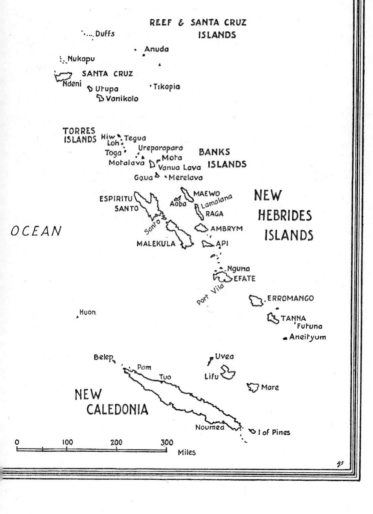

MELANESIA

REEF & SANTA CRUZ
ISLANDS

.·... Duffs

· Anuda

: Nukapu

SANTA CRUZ

Ndeni   ▷ Utupa   · Tikopia

▷ Vanikolo

TORRES
ISLANDS   Hiw ▪· Tegua
Loh ·
Toga ·   Ureparapara   BANKS
Motalava   ▷ᵣ Mota   ISLANDS
Vanua Lava
Gaua ▷ · Merelava

ESPIRITU   ◁ᵒ MAEWO
SANTO   Aoba   Lamalana
Santo   RAGA

OCEAN   ◁ AMBRYM

MALEKULA   ◁ API

·

◁ Nguna
◁ EFATE

Port Vila

◁ ERROMANGO

· Huon   ◁ TANNA
· Futuna
▪ Aneityum

NEW
HEBRIDES
ISLANDS

Belep   ᷣ Uvea
Pam   Lifu ◁
Tuo

NEW   ◁ Mare
CALEDONIA

Noumea   ▷ I of Pines

0   100   200   300
Miles

LIST OF ILLUSTRATIONS

All photographs are reproduced by
courtesy of the Melanesian Mission

CHAPTER ONE

HOUSEMASTER AT NORFOLK ISLAND

NORFOLK Island is a small and lovely island four hundred miles north of New Zealand, set alone in the surrounding seas. It had been a convict settlement and when that was given up it had become the home of the descendants of the Mutineers of the *Bounty*, but a thousand acres had been given to the Anglican Mission for its school there. To this school I went as a teacher in March 1902, and there I was ordained the next year.

The Anglican Mission to Melanesia was founded by George Augustus Selwyn, the first Bishop of New Zealand and one of the greatest missionaries of his time. He had been asked when he was consecrated by the Archbishop of Canterbury to make New Zealand a centre from which Christianity should spread to the islands of the north-west Pacific, then unknown, though the people were reputed to be savage headhunters and cannibals. His plan was very simple—a ship in which to bring boys from those islands to New Zealand, and a school in New Zealand where he would educate them and send them back to teach their own people. In 1840 he already had both, a school, St. John's College at Auckland, and a ship, the *Undine*, of twenty tons. So he set out in this ship, without charts of those unknown and dangerous seas more than a thousand miles to the north, he himself the captain and navigator, with a crew of four, and brought to New Zealand his first five boys.

For the next seventy years this remained the plan of the Mission, but the school was moved to Norfolk Island, where the climate was warmer. John Coleridge Patteson became the first Bishop of Melanesia and followed Selwyn's plan in his ship, the *Southern Cross*. John Selwyn, the son of the founder, became the second Bishop and was followed in 1894 by Cecil Wilson, in whose time the school at Norfolk Island had grown to more than two hundred boys from the New Hebrides, Banks, and Solomon Islands. The people of the islands were still mainly heathen, still cannibals and headhunters, but small Christian schools were springing up in all the islands, taught by the boys trained at Norfolk Island. With the Norfolk Islanders the Melanesian schoolboys were always friends; they played cricket and football with them, and owed them a great deal in many ways; from early days some of the Norfolk Islanders were on the Mission staff. When the school was finally moved in 1919 to the Melanesian Islands we were very loth to part from our Norfolk Island friends.

The island is about seven miles long and three or four miles wide, with high basalt cliffs all round it. Above these is a gently undulating table land, like an English park, dominated by Mt. Pitt, 1,000 feet high at the western end. The climate is ideal, English vegetables and fruit grow well, but also oranges and bananas. It was a lovely setting for the Mission headquarters, which was at the western end, under the shadow of Mt. Pitt. The thousand acres owned by the Mission had been made into a model farm, with cattle, sheep, and horses, and large gardens to supply the boys with the food they were used to in their own islands, such as yams and sweet potatoes and bananas. The boys of the school worked the farm. A road went through the middle of it; on the one side was the group of the boys' houses, the dining-hall, the chapel and the printing and carpentry shops; on the other side the houses of the married members of the staff, with whom lived about thirty or forty Melanesian girls; the sewing room where the boys' clothes were made; the hospital and the big playing fields. You approached the headquarters through a magnificent avenue, a mile long, of Norfolk Island pines, planted by the convicts—unfortunately this was destroyed by the Americans during the Second World War to make an aerodrome.

There were four boys' houses, each in charge of a housemaster; the boys slept on smooth six-foot boards about fifteen inches wide, set upright against the walls by day so that the dormitory became a school room. In each of these buildings the housemaster had two small rooms. The forty or more boys of the house were always in and out of his rooms and some of them looked after him, but all the school met for meals in the large dining-hall in the centre of the quadrangle. At the west end of the dining-hall was the tower with its chiming clock whose sound carried a long way.

But the thing you never forgot was the chapel at the east end of the quadrangle, surely the most beautiful school chapel in the southern hemisphere. Dr. Codrington, Patteson's friend, who was headmaster of St. Barnabas School for twenty years, had designed and built it as a memorial to the Bishop who had been killed at Nukapu Island. It was built of local grey sandstone and held about two hundred boys. The floor was of Devonshire marble and above the altar was a superb carved walnut reredos; above this the famous Burne-Jones windows. The carved seats were set lengthwise in three tiers and were beautifully inlaid with Melanesian shell and mother-of-pearl work; at the west end was a fine rose window. The tattered flags of previous Bishops hung from the walls ("How nice", said a visitor to Bishop Wilson, "when your flag hangs here!"). The bare-foot Melanesians came in without making a sound on the marble floor; you knelt in your seat in an empty chapel and rose to find it full of dark-skinned worshippers. The fine organ had been given by the authoress Charlotte Yonge, the Bishop's cousin, and it was played, and played well, by a succession of Melanesian organists. On the altar stood the lovely silver cross and candlesticks made from Patteson's silver, and here a European or barefoot Melanesian priest celebrated a daily Eucharist.

The beauty and awe of this chapel made a deep impression on generations of schoolboys who worshipped in it. Many came simply to see it and tell their people about it; none ever forgot it; they tried to reproduce something a little like it in their own islands.

Between the houses of the married people and the cliffs were twenty acres of playing fields, where two hundred young Melanesians played cricket and football every day. The Mission had a cricket tradition; Patteson had been Captain of Eton and won the match against Harrow; and Wilson, the first bishop under whom I worked, had been a member of the Kent eleven which was the only county to defeat the Australians, I think in 1884. The soccer eleven would have held its own with New Zealand club sides. When I joined I became games master, and all Norfolk Island old boys will remember many exciting cricket and football matches with the Norfolk Islanders or the Europeans at the cable station.

Half a mile from the school were the large gardens which supplied us with food. Europeans and Melanesians worked these together daily after morning school, clearing, weeding and planting. We also kept in order five miles of island roads and sometimes we had what were called "working holidays", i.e. instead of school we worked from 8 a.m. to 5 p.m. on the gardens or roads. Some boys also learnt to milk and look after the cattle, sheep and horses; others worked in the printing and carpentry shops; others did the cooking. About a dozen boys cooked each week, with a white man at the head of them, who was usually someone fresh from Oxford or Cambridge who had never cooked in his life before, but he happened to be the last to join the staff. In my first six months I was cook.

The school customs were those instituted by the first headmaster, Lonsdale Pritt, when the Mission school was in Auckland. The boys were divided into fifteen to twenty "cook sets"; at the head of each was a "head cook", or prefect, with a "mate" (these always from different islands). At the beginning of a school term the whole school assembled in the dining-hall and the head cooks and mates sat at their several tables and proceeded in turn to choose their men from the crowd standing at the far end of the hall. Then it was a bad time for boys who had shown themselves to be lazy; they would be left to the last, standing sheepishly among the small fry and the new boys. After morning school the boys fell in and were sent out to work, each set to its particular job. Boys came to the school for two years and then had a holiday in their islands; some remained at the school for as much as ten or twelve years.

Lonsdale Pritt had made Mota the lingua franca of the school and it remained so for all our schools for more than seventy years. It is the language of a small island in the Banks Group and because of its use for so long by the Mission it has become, next to Fijian, the best known of the Melanesian languages. Pritt chose it because it was the only one he knew himself, but as it happened there could not have been a better choice. At St. Barnabas, Norfolk Island, no English was spoken and all the teaching was in Mota. All the members of the school staff spoke it fluently and boys from other islands learnt it very quickly. It was a good foundation for learning other Melanesian languages later. A new member of the staff learnt it quickly because he heard nothing else spoken, because he had to teach in it, and because when he was working on the farm with the boys and looking after them in his house, he was hearing it all the time and using it of necessity in school, at work, and in the playing fields.

Two days after I arrived the headmaster took me into a classroom in which forty boys were sitting, twenty on each side of a long table with a blackboard at the end of it. "This is your class", he said. "Go ahead"—and left me to it. It was a lesson on the New Testament. The boys and I looked solemnly at one another; they knew no English, I no Mota, except one word which had chanced to catch my eye in the Mota dictionary—*manaranara*, bloody—but it seemed difficult to give a lesson with only that word. It was like throwing a boy into deep water to teach him to swim. I think I wrote a parable from the Mota Bible on the blackboard and told them to copy it. But every day I did better. A good linguist usually hears a new language before he can speak it, but I was speaking it even before I could hear it well.

I was given charge at once of Codrington House with thirty boys in it. The bell for bed went at 9.30 and the housemaster went in and said Compline with the boys already lying on their six-foot boards and curled up in their blue blankets. Then next morning when the bell went at 6.30 he went in to see that all were up and about. All you could see on most of the boards was a pile of blue blankets and you did not know at which end to poke tentatively, since the boy might be sleeping either way on his board. Miss Yonge, in her life of Patteson, describes how the Bishop used to go into the dormitory in the morning and pull the blankets off the boys "with shouts of merry laughter". This method may be a good one for the saints, but not for a young housemaster. It is better to let sleeping dogs lie. In the beginning I did once try something of the sort, and the sleeping dog suddenly became a raging tiger, leaping at me and wrestling with me round the dormitory. These boys were the sons of cannibals and headhunters, and not far below the surface in those days was a hot and fierce temper.

The boys were certainly different in some ways from the boys I had taught in New Zealand. Soon after I got there I saw one day a lad from Mala, for long the wildest island of the Solomons, cutting down with an axe a post of the large gate leading into the school grounds. I felt unwilling to interfere with a young man from Mala wielding an axe, but I drew the attention of a senior missionary to what he was doing. "Leave him alone", I was told. "He has a grievance and wants to let us all know it. He will be all right again when he has finished with the gate post." No doubt it is a satisfactory way of expressing a grievance, but I felt it would not be allowed in a school at home, and I decided not to provoke too much the lads from Mala.

With me from New Zealand had come another young New Zealand schoolmaster,* and George and I felt our way along together. On our first Sunday we walked up into the school gardens and came upon a lot of ripe melons. "Wild, of course," said George, leading me astray, and we set to work on them. Next morning in the hall the headmaster asked the masters and boys to remain when breakfast was over as he had something to say to the boys. The Rev. T. C. Cullwick, the headmaster, was a very big man and a stern disciplinarian. He began walking up and down the hall, talking rapidly in Mota and apparently getting more and more angry, while the boys looked more and more alarmed. It became a torrent of violent Mota of which, of course, I understood not one word, so I whispered to my neighbour: "What is he talking about?" and he whispered back: "The boys have been stealing the melons in the school gardens." The headmaster was in full spate as I got up hastily and said: "Sir, it was George and me." He turned, stared at me for a moment and burst into a roar of laughter in which the whole school gladly joined.

What a headmaster he was! The best I have known. The boys

* He later became Canon Coats, of Auckland.

called him Matches because he flared up so quickly yet died down so soon. In the islands the people called him *Lang vus*, Cyclone; and he could be like that, though he was generally jovial and full of fun. When he was angry even the lads from Mala were afraid of him. He could not put up with slackness or rudeness or cruelty but was tolerant of some things which many missionaries think to be worse, and he was tender and understanding with any boy who was in trouble. He could flare up in a moment. At fall-in one day he suddenly went for a boy for something or other and the boy dashed up a loquat tree near by with T.C.C. after him shouting "*Siwo ma! Siwo ma!*—Come down! Come down!" while at each shout the boy went higher and faster. Then from T.C.C. came a roar of laughter and all was over. Another day he was on his way to his house along a slippery clay path, with a pile of books in his arms. He slipped and fell heavily, the books flying in all directions and a boy following him began a laugh just as T.C.C. looked round and glared at him. This is the only time I have seen a laugh frozen rigid on someone's face.

T.C.C. left a deep impression on all the boys who passed through the school. When, in later years in the islands, you met a teacher who plodded on faithfully, sticking to his job in spite of all difficulties and sometimes real dangers and never giving in, you generally found he had been at Norfolk Island under T.C.C.

But the boys at St. Barnabas were not always easy to control in those days and from time to time their wild nature would break out. One Christmas Eve a little New Hebridean stabbed a little Mala boy during a quarrel and blood flowed. In less than five minutes some one hundred and fifty Solomon Islanders had thrown off all their clothes and, stark naked, seized axes, knives, spears, anything that came to hand, and were in full cry after some sixty New Hebrideans, who for their part were going all out for the sea coast. It was an exciting time for housemasters. Below the school grounds were a number of small houses, one belonging to each island, where the boys used to cook the fish they caught, and smoke, and enjoy themselves. The armed and naked Solomon Islanders rushed for those owned by the New Hebrideans to slaughter anyone they could find in them—but they were all quickly empty except for one in which a quiet New Hebridean "head cook" sat smoking. As the Solomon Islanders rushed down to it they shouted, "Anyone in there?" and the New Hebridean very wisely shouted "No!" and the Solomon Islanders rushed on past it, to the relief of a housemaster who felt helpless to do anything. These riots were not common but they did occur from time to time. On this occasion it was T.C.C. who quelled it, by the vigorous use of a stockwhip.

The school grounds had been made beautiful by St. Barnabas' former headmaster, Dr. Codrington, not only a great ethnologist and linguist, but also a great gardener. I had his house and garden and greenhouse and was as fond of flowers as he had been, and like him was much troubled by the snails which infested the flower garden. I asked a lad who had been his gardener how he had dealt with them. Joe said the Doctor used to give the boys sixpence to collect a bucket of snails and bring them to him.

"And then how did he destroy them?" I asked.

"He didn't," said Joe. "We always put them back in the garden for the other boys."

The Doctor had no ear at all for music and could not recognise a tune, yet he wrote the finest hymns in the Mota hymnbook, perfect in rhythm, whereas Patteston's hymns were lacking in this, although he had a perfect ear—a peculiarity I have noticed in others. The Doctor was the greatest philologist and anthropologist Melanesia has known. He was headmaster for twenty years and the chief translator of the Mota Bible, which is one of the best versions, in fine Mota prose, and he was an incomparable teacher. He compiled the grammars of thirty-six Melanesian languages with the help of boys at the school. St. Barnabas was very fortunate in its three great headmasters, Codrington, Palmer, and Cullwick, for a headmaster makes or mars a school.

At Christmas time every year came the dances and the production of plays by the boys. The Mission has always encouraged native dancing and at Christmas two great piles of firewood were built up near the hospital, about twenty yards apart. At eight o'clock in the evening these were lit and steadily replenished during the next four hours or so, and the staff and Europeans living on the island gathered to see the dancing. Groups of dancers from each island in turn came in to dance between the fires. The New Hebridean dances were often dramas telling a story, rather like those of Bali. The Solomon Island dances usually imitated fishing, hunting, or fighting. In the old days dancing parties used to travel about from village to village, and often it was exciting for the spectators as the dancers had weapons concealed and would suddenly fall on the spectators in the middle of the dance and slaughter them. In the usual Gela dance the dancers were four abreast and danced crouching low, with shield in the left hand and spear in the right, leaping forward, backward, and sideways and grunting as they danced. When they practised this on Gela the old women of the village gathered round with long poles and whacked any young man not crouching low enough. As the dance took about thirty minutes, and the dancers worked themselves up, it was quite exhausting. One Christmas I got Nat, our painter, to brown me all over, and arrayed as a Gela warrior I danced in the front row. It took many hours of practice beforehand.

During December the boys used to practise the dances half the night on the playing fields after the bell for bed. It was during this month that we had our worst epidemics and we housemasters used often to spend our nights in the hospital watching over sick or dying boys and listening to the plaintive music of the dancing parties in the nearby playing fields. Sister Kate presided over the hospital during the day. One night, however, she was alone in the hospital and, going in to see the patients, was chased round the ward by a sick boy with a carving knife. She dashed into her room, locked the door, leaned out of the window and rang a large bell about 2 a.m. We all turned out on that dark night to search for the Solomon Islander with the carving knife, who was wandering about at large. We found him in a deep ditch half a mile from the hospital, and his nocturnal wandering cured him of pneumonia.

For sixty years and more St. Barnabas turned out hundreds of young Christian teachers. If education means mental and moral training they got this in good measure through the Mota language.

17

I doubt if the lads of any later schools have known their Bibles as these did. They worshipped daily in that wonderful chapel. Their homes were still wild and savage and many of them were wild young men when they came but they were fine material, and in after years the pioneer teachers of the Melanesians, the foundation on which the church of Melanesia has been built. Few of them are alive now, but they were good stuff.

CHAPTER TWO

THE CHILDREN

IN 1903 I went to Mota in the Banks Islands, chiefly to hear the language we used at Norfolk Island in its own home, for there they spoke it with a different intonation, a lilt absent from our Norfolk Island Mota, and there were many more words than we used. While I was there I collected about a thousand words not found in the Mota dictionary, which contains about eight thousand words though there must be double that number in the language. The Arosi language has about thirty thousand.

At Mota I first came to know Melanesian children, the same in all the islands, and always something to delight a man's heart. Most of the time I lived with them and played their native games with them. You can learn a Melanesian language best from the children. They speak more clearly than their elders, and you can ask the latter questions afterwards.

What glorious places these islands are for children to grow up in! I know very well the black side—the fear, the cruelty, the sickness; all that has been said so often, especially by missionaries stressing the need for missionary work, but the other side is forgotten, though there is another side.

Melanesia is a playground for children. The sea and the reefs are full of innumerable strange and beautiful creatures of all sorts of shapes and colours, and they can wander at will and collect what they like. They can shoot the fish with bow and arrow, or the big spiders, which are so hard to catch in any other way. After shooting the fish in the pools on the reef they can go and cook and eat them, and many kinds of shell fish too are good eating. You do see most wonderful and beautiful and strange things in the pools on the reefs.

Then behind the village come the low hills of the Ma-tanga, the "middle" ground between the village and the high mountains.

Here are their gardens. And beyond these again the forest-covered mysterious mountains where anything might live. I remember coming to a small lake of brownish water on the high hills of Mala, and standing on the grassy bank that surrounded it and gazing into the water. Suddenly about twelve yards out appeared a bony hand, as of a skeleton, lifted out of the lake. It seemed to have its fingers crooked, shutting and opening again as it came through the water towards me in a most menacing way. I stood my ground rather uncertainly, till it got near enough for me to see its body dimly through the brown water. The body was only about half the size of the skeleton-like hand and arm. I never knew what it was, for it moved away again, rather to my relief.

But it is not only creatures like this that you may come across. The children believe in strange beings of all sorts, some like our fairies, some good, some bad and dangerous. In our own childhood we thought of magic as something splendid and strange. The owner of a cap could put it on and become invisible, because it was a magic cap; in an enchanted castle anything might happen; a magic lantern was more than an ordinary lantern, it brought beautiful pictures before us. The world was full of magic. The Melanesian world is full of magic too; but they call it mana—a word in all the Banks Island and Solomon Island languages*. All mana comes from spiritual beings. It is not a material thing; all the mana in the world could be put into a small betel nut, so they told me. It can give prosperity, can harm or heal, it is dangerous to come near it carelessly (like a live wire) but it can be powerful to help you. You might come across it anywhere, in persons, in stones, in weapons, in strange creatures; the Melanesian world is full of it. And in this world the Melanesian children grow up, a world where anything may happen; a world in which Europeans, who have lost the sense of wonder, no longer dwell. I have heard Europeans who are not Christians referred to as pagans, but that is a slander on pagans, for these Europeans are materialists and no pagan is as bad as that.

* The same name is found in Fijian and Polynesian; other forms are the Arosi *mena* and the Ulava *namana*. When you get out of the area of Austronesian languages [see Appendix] you lose the word and perhaps the idea, though that is wider than the word.

The children in Mota, or in Arosi in the Solomons, believe in many mysterious beings. As I know the Arosi people best, I shall use their names. There were *adaro*—a ghost, or a bird or animal supposed to be the ancestor of the clan and so not to be eaten; but also anything very unusual or strange, such as a white cuscus, or monster eel, or probably, when they first saw them, white people. There were many stories about *adaro* and such like, told to the children by their grandmothers. I wrote down more than one hundred. You can get these stories best from boys.

Besides *adaro* there are *kakamora* and *masi*. These are little beings, about two or three feet tall. The *masi* were always doing foolish things!* They were small people, clever workmen when working for normal folk, but when living among themselves they always managed to make a mess of things and seemed very stupid; and the big folk laughed at them and told many stories about their doings.

Some of them who lived by the sea-shore once found some bait for catching porpoises. So they said to one another, "Come, let us launch the big canoe and go and catch a porpoise". So they got their canoe ready for fishing, and launched it, and six of them paddled as hard as they could out to sea.

The one in the bow happened to look down into the water and there he saw a sunbeam. "Friends," he said, "here is a *dahi*," (which is a crescent-shaped mother-of-pearl ornament hung round the neck). "Stop paddling! all back water! I think we can get it."

They all looked down, sitting very still, and saw the sunbeam in the water, which they thought was a *dahi*. "Yes," they said, "we can dive down and get it."

The one in the bow said to them, "Steady the canoe with your paddles while I dive down for it." So they all kept their paddles stiff to steady the canoe and down he dived, but he could not get hold of the sunbeam. So the second one tried, but he could not get hold of it either. They all tried but none of them could get hold of the sunbeam.

So they paddled back again to the shore and searched for rocks with a hole in them and got some tough creepers to tie to the

* They may be far-off degenerate descendants of the Hobbits, of Professor Tolkien.

21

rocks and set off again, and when they had paddled out to the deep water there was the sunbeam they had seen just as it was before.

So they all held their paddles stiff again and steadied the canoe, and the one in the bow prepared to dive. They tied a rock to his foot and let him down by the creeper over the side of the canoe, and he said to them, "Friends, it is likely you will have to wait about here a long while; getting the *dahi* is going to be hard work."

Down he went with the weight of the rock, deeper and deeper, and they waited and waited, but he never came up again. They watched the bubbles coming to the surface and said to one another, "Give him time and he is sure to get it."

At last the second one said, "I had better go and help him, he is having a hard job;" so he too had a large rock tied to his foot and was let down over the side by the creeper and they said to one another, "The two of them ought to do the job."

But he did not come up again either, so each of them in turn went to help him; but nothing ever came up but the bubbles where the six *masi* were drowned, diving for the sunbeam.

Another time one of them, while looking for eels in a stream, found a frog and took it for his wife. He took her home and set her to cook taro for his dinner. Putting the taro on the fire to broil he went and sat in the men's house chewing betel nut and when he went home, hungry for his meal, the taro was burnt to cinders. He struck the frog in his anger and she fled into a stone outside. Very angry he went to the stone and said, "Where is your daughter? Give her to me." The stone said nothing. So he seized his spear and club and attacked the stone, breaking both his weapons on it, without disturbing the frog inside. Full of anger and despair he returned to his home without his wife, whom he never saw again.

The *kakamora* are not unlike the *masi* but more mischievous. They are the little folk of the mountains, sometimes only two feet tall, very dark or very fair, with no weapons but long finger-nails with which they stab. They build no houses, have no tools, make no fires, but they are very strong and live in holes or caves. They have an unknown language and imitate Melanesian talk, but all wrong. They have straight hair, usually like Europeans. They dance in the moonlight and the rain. They love to make fun of men and delude them. Perhaps you are looking for something, and you go to a place where you are quite sure you put it, but it is not there; a *kakamora* has moved it. This has often happened to myself when I lived where *kakamora* are found, though I never saw one.

But once I very nearly did see one. I was called in great excitement to see the fresh footprint of one on the river bank. It was a very small footprint and did not belong to anyone of the village—and that was true, for everyone can recognise the footprint of anyone within ten miles of his village, I have tested them again and again. I remember once at Pamua we were playing the game where half the boys go out and the other half try to stop them getting in. It was a moonlight night. A few boys stood near the main road with a lantern. One of the other side tried to get in, dressed as a Government policeman, with a mailbag on his shoulder (that was how our mail came), and the boys guarding the path put the lantern, not as we should have done to his face, but to his feet, and knew him at once. Another time I was crossing the island with a guide and he left me suddenly to follow a footprint he didn't know, and he followed it for some miles till he found out. So I was very near that day to seeing a *kakamora*, one of these mischievous little folk. I am very small myself, and *kakamora* was a name given to me by my friends.

You may come across an *adaro* without seeing it. I once smelt one—a strange and horrible smell that came suddenly from nowhere with nothing to cause it, and passed swiftly—just an *adaro* passing by, I was told. A rainbow is dangerous because it is the pathway of the *adaro*, and full of them. Then at the end of Arosi at a headland where it can be very rough, a great fish, a ray, comes to your boat or canoe (I often saw it swim to us), and if you sacrifice to it you get fine weather. I did not sacrifice to it, but with the tail of my eye I once saw my crew giving it some of my tea, and we had fine weather.

Then there is the *adaro here* of Arosi, called in Mota a *mae valeleas*, and in the Reef Islands of the Solomons *atua fafine*. This generally appears to a man on the shore as a beautiful woman (to a woman, I think, as a handsome young man). One day at Mota I was sitting talking to a group of people among whom was a woman named Mary. A man rushed up in great excitement; he had just met Mary on the beach, and knew she was not Mary because she had red and white flowers in her hair and women only put flowers of one colour. It was of course an *adaro here*, who had been careless of details. An *adaro here* is very dangerous. R. L. Stevenson describes one in his *Beach of Falesa*.

There are terrible *adaro*, called *adaro ni matawa*, dreaded foreign beings of the ocean (*matawa*), who kill men in canoes by spearing them. Melanesians love to draw them, half human, half fish. And in the forests are *mumu* (in Gela *mumutambu*), gigantic wild men with hairy bodies, straight hair and long nails. And there are great serpent spirits, who were the creators, and incarnate in sacred snakes; and many, many other strange beings. Altogether a most exciting world for a child to live in, a world full of wonders and the unknown.

This is a very long digression. I had meant to write of the children's games. Nearly every game has a song, like our "Nuts in May". In the game called in Mota *Gisigisi*, one player goes off and sits a few yards from the rest and shuts his eyes. Then one of the others goes to him quietly and gently touches him; if he can recognise by the touch who it is, that player must take his place. As each one makes his venture they all sing:

> Gisigisi
> Gis pepewu save
> Gis pepewu oleole
> Ol Rowo, gis matangtang
> Me gisia! (he's touched him!)

At the words: *Me gisia!* they all shout out, he touches the sitter, and the latter guesses who it is. The words of the song are in an archaic form of the Mota language, and so are the Arosi or Gela songs, and sometimes the meaning of these song words is not now known. The children themselves had a secret language of their own (by matathesis of words) which they fondly believed their elders could not follow, forgetting that they too had once been children. At Kwaravae on Mala the grown-up people all transposed the syllables of the language as written in their books, so that church services were quite different from the ordinary talk of the people.

In another Mota game called *Sorasorav* (*sora* means to stroke), they begin by sitting in a circle, legs stretched out and feet meeting in the centre, and they stroke their legs while they sing a song. After several actions, and a song for each of them, they are sitting each with his legs doubled up under him. Each rises; if his joints crack as he does so, then he is a flying fox (*qarat*); if they don't he is a hermit crab (*gatou*). The hermit crabs go off to the beach, and the flying foxes towards the mountain. One of the hermit crabs strikes another who gives a yell, and then all the flying foxes call out, "Who are you there?"

"The children of the hermit crabs are we," they all chant.

"What are you doing down there?" say the flying foxes; to which the hermit crabs reply with many insulting remarks as to what they will do with the heads of the flying foxes. The flying foxes go through the same ritual and insult the hermit crabs. It ends in a wild romp as the hermit crabs and flying foxes rush backwards into each other, trying to knock each other down, shouting and laughing. These and many other games I used to play with the Mota children.

In Arosi on San Cristoval the children would wake at dawn but not get up, and each lying on his sleeping mat would begin crooning:

Dangi, dangi, dangisi rarua	Daylight, daylight, shine on those two
Rua wae rarua	Two old women there
Raru beriberi bua. . . .	Stealing the betel nut. . . .

Quite a long song, sung very softly by the little brown mites. Then they would get up, blow on the embers of the almost dead fire on the stone hearth till it glowed, and sit round it chatting and warming themselves, for a cold breeze would be coming down the river valley. One would be holding his hands over the fire, and the others would put their hands over his and press them down, singing:

Boiboki eu	Cover his hand on the fire.
Iatei mai eu?	Who is in the fire?
Ia wae kehukehu.	Old Mother sitting tight.

And then, warmed up, they would sit on the beam along the low beds and slap their thighs and sing another song, have a snack from green bananas broiled in their skins on the embers, and then out into the new day. They were always singing; if they saw a yam more red than usual, or found a megapod's egg in the sand, or anything else unusual, they made a song about it. They sang children's charms for rain or fine weather; they played, and they very rarely quarrelled. Sometimes it was a grimmer game of making an oven in the sand and bringing in a captive to roast in the oven, but always with a song.

If the children were left alone in the house they would wonder, with delicious fear, whether some strange thing, *kakamora* or *adaro*, might come into the house while mother was away. These beings use ashes instead of lime when chewing betel nut. So the children fill a half coconut shell with ashes, put some betel pepper leaf, a bit of betel nut, and a little stick in the coconut cup, put this outside the door, come in and shut the door fast, and lie very still under their mats with shining eyes, wondering, if perhaps a *kakamora* or *masi* or *adaro* will come, and chanting softly a magic song to bring him: *kukuru masi.* When mother comes back they throw off their mats and rush out to look at the coconut cup. Yes, the ashes are red. He came! How lucky the door was fast!

How much more I could write about the children! Their early childhood was a happy time. They were rarely punished; the Melanesians view with horror our punishment of children. They helped their parents in the gardens, but had lots of time for play, and no school. Now they go to school and learn reading, writing and *figas* and their catechism; perhaps they are told that their grandmothers' tales of *kakamora* are all nonsense; they don't sing the old songs or play the old games as they used to do; there is not so much mystery and magic; it is the new Melanesia. I liked them the way they were.

When I was living on Mota the boys often took me at night to the top of the hill to see the sun rise. Mota is a volcanic island with a raised limestone plateau round a central cone about 1,000 feet high. We climbed in the dark through the forest and stood there watching the sun rise, with all the islands spread out before us, in the far distance the northern New Hebrides. At the top was a deep volcanic vent, bottomless the boys said, the *Sura*, the road by which the dead went to the underworld. (There is one on Gela too.) I was made to stretch my hands over it, with the two first fingers close together, and then the boys bound them with creepers, and chanted:

"*Naqongimu ni qoqo a marama*—May your days be many in the land of light."

This was to give me a long life in the islands, and there must be something in this magic, for I have had nearly sixty years! Then we would *aleg* (shout for joy) and all rush shouting down the sides of the mountain.

In an article in the Mission magazine, the *Southern Cross Log*, Dr. Welchman, who loved to watch the Melanesian games, gives a true picture of Melanesian children at play; the bright moonlight, the white coral sand, the chanting (always in every game), the spirit of fun, the delight in absurdity, the powers of invention. So in the evenings they play for hours. This Bugotu game is called Dukonio:

"It is a lovely night," he writes, "the moon is nearly full, there is no wind beyond a gentle breeze; and the waves are just rippling, no more, on the sandy beach. The tide is low enough to leave a good broad strip, and here two lines of children are seated, facing each other, about five yards apart. One boy in the middle of the row has a long stick and is giving directions to his party, who are squatting in a line. Now they are all ready and they begin. The leader thumps the ground with his stick to beat time. As he beats they all chant:

Dukonio faafarakonio	Dukonio faafarakonio
Vano me mai gua	Come here someone
Jimi ma taugna	Jimi᾿ or his wife
Mai hatia gua	Come and take away
Supa tidatho eni	This wizard's staff
Ke fuofuro eni	It is rubbed with scent
Ke nainali eni	It smells beautiful
Ke jena sirakugna	The rings have jingled
Ke tangi na selelegna	The beads have rattled
Mai ohoa gua	Come and take it away

Sometimes they vary the name Jimi, but that is immaterial so long as they chant lustily and wind up with a little yell for the last note, and give a vigorous thump to show they are ready to be attacked. They are all sitting solemn and stolid, looking straight in front of them. There is a little pause. A nice-mannered quiet little girl is pushed forward by the opposite leader, and she walks quietly across and says:

"Give me the stick."

She is so proper she would say "please", only there is no such word in Bugotu. The boy with the staff looks up, first at the stick and then at the sky, and says:

"I won't give you the stick; it is very precious, I told Martin to go and get me this, and he climbed up the tree, and this fell down, and I took it and rubbed it over with scent, and it is mine. Go away again."

The little girl goes back to her place without it, for no-one has laughed. She was much too well-behaved.

The chant begins again; another pause; and this time a boy comes out of his own accord—it surely must be Jimi himself. He does not walk gently up; he goes across jumping on his haunches like a frog, and squatting opposite the leader he says roughly:

"Give me that stick."

But the whole side sit gazing into space without even a smile, while the leader says:

"I won't give it to you; I told my dog to fetch me a stick, and he barked at the moon, and this fell down, and I've ornamented it, and rubbed it to smell nice, and now I shall keep it. Go away."

While he has been talking no-one has laughed or even smiled, so the stick still stays where it is and Jimi has to go back discomfited.

A third time the chant is finished, and now another boy is sent. He does not walk properly either, for he lies on the ground full length and swims across with a side-stroke, and an occasional kick of the legs. This is beginning to tell; and when he gets across he doesn't go to the leader, who is a practised hand, but addresses himself to a neighbour whose face is already breaking down and with a cracked voice and a face drawn to one side, asks for the stick. Before the leader can speak the laugh has come, and John walks off triumphantly with the treasure, which he gives to his leader.

Now the other side begins the chant, looking determined to keep the stick. Not so fast; there are knowing hands in the first lot; and a biggish boy comes out walking on all fours, not on his hands and feet, but literally on the tip of his toes and fingers; his back is arched and his head out; he looks just like a cat in a temper, and you almost expect to see his tail. Half way across he gives a wriggle and a spring into the air, like a lamb at play, and all at once the chanters laugh out loud; it was too much for them altogether, and Pande carries off the stick—he has no need to ask for it. So it goes on backwards and forwards. Sometimes they can keep their faces and the stick; sometimes they lose their gravity, and their prize together. They do not seem to keep any score. The two words at the beginning are mere play words; if they ever had any meaning it has been lost."

This is also a Gela game, called *Lavi koni* on that island; *koni* is said to mean "destitute".

Melanesians, and especially Melanesian children, are much closer to animals than we are. They are often cruel to them, but so they are to human beings; yet they look on animals as brothers, and when they read about St. Francis it is not his poverty that attracts them, but his love of animals. The stories told by children are more often than not about animals acting like men, and animals come into almost all their stories. They expect them to behave like men—like foolish men very often. The children know all their habits and their characters.

Once upon a time all the animals went on a sea voyage, among them a pig, a dog, a flying fox, a hermit crab, a mosquito and several kinds of birds. Their canoe was the broad leaf of a large sort of taro. No one had paddles, they liked just to drift about singing songs. The dog was in charge of the party and made each sing in turn, but he found fault with all of them. The cockatoo tried, but the dog said his voice was horrible; it was the same with the parrot and the pig and all the others; none of them were any good, said the dog. But at last a bird sang beautifully but without any words, just beautiful notes.

"Sing that again," said the dog, "but put words to your song this time."

So the bird sang, and his song was all about the dog:

> "You lazy dog! all your desire
> Is to lie by the side of the fire;
> Into your belly you cram
> Bones or a burnt bit of yam.
> Your teeth are so long, and your nose
> Is as funny and queer as your toes.
> You follow the men if they call,
> And bark for no reason at all!"

The dog got more and more angry and began biting the leaf till their canoe broke. The birds all flew away, but the rest of the animals fell into the water. The pig swam to the shore, and the hermit crab sank to the bottom and began to crawl and got ashore after three years; the dog himself swam ashore and the mosquito settled inside the dog's ear and so came ashore dry, flying out of the dog's ear when they landed.

"Dear me, friend," said the dog, "how did you keep so dry?"

"Your ear," said the mosquito.

"What!" said the dog.

"Your ear," said the mosquito.

"You brute," said the dog, and chased the mosquito. But a crab had made a hole there and the mosquito flew into it.

"Please let me hide," said the mosquito to the crab. "The dog is after me and means to kill me."

"Come inside, friend," said the crab. "I will see to the dog."

The dog was digging at the hole and put his nose to it, and the crab seized his nose and held him fast.

The story goes on with more adventures of the dog. If you sit with the children on the white beach in the moonlight they will tell you all sorts of stories about the animals and their adventures. This particular story, from Ysabel, was told by the late George Bogesi,* who was one of my Norfolk Island schoolboys.

* In *Oceania*, March, 1948.

CHAPTER THREE

ST. MICHAEL'S SCHOOL, PAMUA

I FIRST went to San Cristoval in 1908 and began to learn something of the people; but it was not till 1910 that the bishop asked me to begin a school for small boys at Pamua, which had been the headquarters of the missionary working on the island. He had now gone to Bungana, a small island off Gela, to start a similar school there. These were the first of our boarding-schools for small boys in the Solomons, although eighteen years earlier there had been, for a short time, a school for older lads at Siota, the pioneer school in the Group.

I was set down at Pamua by the Mission ship, which then went off to look for boys for my school from San Cristoval, Ulawa and Mala, the three large islands of the eastern Solomons, while I went on to Rafufafu, a village about a mile away, to wait for the boys. I had to be led into the village, which was surrounded by pitfalls because they were expecting an attack. These were deep holes, with sharp stakes at the bottom, each covered with twigs and grass, and there was only one safe way through them to the village. They told me to sleep in the chief's house. I felt rather nervous about the attack they were expecting.

"When will it be?" I asked them.

"Any time, very likely tonight."

"And what part of the village will they attack?"

"The chief's house, of course."

I slept rather uneasily, but there was no attack.

After some days the ship brought me twenty small boys, and we made a leaf house for them just beyond my own house, which was a small European one on tall piles. Pamua is on the shore, with a white beach of coral sand. A woman named Pamua was once murdered there, hence the name.

San Cristoval was at that time still a cannibal island. It is perhaps a libel on the Solomon Islanders to call them all cannibals. Even the people of Malaita were not cannibals in the worst sense. It is true that after killing people they sometimes ate them, but that was only to show they despised them and had conquered them completely. You leave no doubt about your superiority when you kill and eat your enemy. It was just that, not to get the *mana* of their victims. The people of Gela and Ysabel say they never ate human flesh, though I rather doubt this. I do not know if the people of New Georgia and the islands to the west were cannibals. What they practised was head-hunting. It was a hobby of theirs to collect human heads and preserve them, so they went to other islands looking for people's heads to add to their collection; but it was just a hobby, as you might collect stamps or shells.*

The people of San Cristoval really were cannibals. They liked human flesh, and they did not think a feast was complete without it. When you went among the hill people in those days they offered you human flesh; and they had a market at one end of the island where they fattened up people for feasts. But at the same time I found them very nice people. It is a mistake to think that cannibals cannot be nice people. Some vegetarians are very nice people. It is all a matter of taste!

They had professional murderers, who provided a body for a feast. These were quite different from the *ramo* of Malaita, who would kill anyone for money, and were mere killers, savage and fierce fighters. The professional murderers of San Cristoval were quite genial people. I knew one of them named Sam very well. I met him once near his village, on the other side of the island; he had come down to the shore and we had quite a long talk. Feeling interested in a profession new to me on its technical side, I asked Sam how he did it.

"Oh," said Sam, "it is quite easy; you go to some village and chum up with some fellow—help him in his garden, go everywhere with him; then one day when you and he are alone you kill him and go off with his body in your canoe."

* No doubt it had social significance; you cannot lightly do away with even such things without giving something in their place. In the old "blackbirding" days the New Zealand captains of the recruiting ships used to chase canoes in the eastern Solomons and cut off the heads of the people in them to sell to the headhunters of the western Solomons. These New Zealanders (and Australians) the people called the "white headhunters".

C

I asked him how many people he had killed, for feasts, in this way. Sam thought and said: "Sixty-four—up to now." I didn't quite like "up to now", being so near Sam's village, and presently he said: "You know, I have taken quite a fancy to you. How about coming and stopping with me in my village for a week or two?" But I felt I must get on. Sam was a very pleasant and a very dangerous person.

The missionary before me once had a difference with Sam. Sam had taken one of my friend's schoolboys in this way and gone off with the body in his canoe. My friend launched his whale-boat and gave chase for about twenty miles. When the wind squalls came the boat gained on the canoe, and when the wind fell Sam gained; it was neck and neck. But at last the breeze became steady and Sam saw it was hopeless. He paddled into a little bay, laid the body on the beach and made off. My friend sailed in, buried the boy in a village nearby and returned triumphantly home. This was one of Sam's failures and must have worried him.

The school began well, the boys sleeping in their leaf house, just below our ten-foot high verandah. But there were all sorts of difficulties at first. A party of men came and camped in the forest about a mile away. They wanted to get one of my boys for a feast—not, of course, as a guest. With me was a Melanesian teacher from the Banks Islands, and we had to stop up every night with a loaded shot gun, watching over our boys. He took one half of the night and I took the other. This went on for about two months, and then our visitors got tired and went away; but we always had to be careful.

A great many hill people used to come down to work for us for tobacco—stick tobacco, you bought twenty-six sticks for a shilling in those days. Sometimes we would have eighty hill men in the school grounds, wild-looking fellows armed with spears and clubs. We had to make a rule that they should leave their weapons on the other side of our boundary stream, otherwise we might all have been killed suddenly on the whim of some man. At first they did not always obey the rule, and one day when I saw a man stalking about with a spear in front of our house, I went down and spoke to him and he tried to spear me. We had a wrestle together before I managed to break the spear; then he jumped back, drew a big knife and crouched to spring. I did not know the book of words for this, and wondered what to do next. We glared at one another and then he put his knife back and stalked off, leaving the broken spear on the ground. After that they kept the rule.

Sometimes there were other alarms. War canoes from Mala used to go along the coast looking for someone to kill, or they might be our own San Cristoval canoes. One day we saw two war canoes, about twenty armed men in each, going over to Ugi island eight miles away to kill the white trader there. They had spears and long handled tomahawks, very dangerous weapons with handles about five feet long. (The native name is kilakila—not a corruption of an English word.) Fortunately the trader was away in his boat, and so they contented themselves with looting his house and store and burning them down. We heard about it, and that they were going to call on us on their way home, not to harm us, just to have a meal and a rest. However we could not allow such a party at our Mission school. Early next morning the two canoes paddled into our bay, and our thirty schoolboys retired to the hill behind. I went down to the sandy beach (feeling rather lonely) and waded out to meet the canoes. I asked them what they had come for. "Just a spell," they said. I told them we knew all about them and what they had done and we did not allow people like them in a Mission school. They got very excited, and some of them jumped out of their canoes and stood round me waving their kilakila and shouting. It was very interesting —but all bluff. Presently they got into their canoes again and paddled away; but such things upset the routine of a school.

There were other things too. There was a chief named Wakerem-wara (Wakere for short) who lived in a village about ten miles up in the hills and he was always sending messages down that he was coming to kill us all. These old chiefs were fine old men and they were very punctilious about telling you when they were coming to kill you, four o'clock next Thursday, or something like that. He didn't come, but the schoolboys were nervous, and I thought the only way was to go up and see him. So when the Archdeacon came on his ketch the Selwyn I asked him to come up with me. He jumped at it. Archdeacons are very nice people, and this one was no exception—a young Englishman just out and quite new to the islands. He had been made Archdeacon of the Solomons while still a curate in England. This was his first visitation and he was not yet tanned with the sun like the rest of us.

The way to Wakere's village was up a river; sometimes wading in the river bed over big boulders against a strong rush of water, very often falling down with a splash; sometimes following a narrow track in the forest on one side or the other; continually crossing and recrossing the river. Unfortunately that day it rained a deluge, coming down in sheets hour after hour, and presently the river was in high flood and quite impossible to cross. The Melanesians with us had to cut a track with their long knives as best they could along the northern bank. It was slow work. It rained and rained, but it was quite warm and we took off our clothes and gave them to our boys to carry. I was fairly brown, but the Archdeacon, fresh from England was very white and beautiful if not very happy. We came to a side stream, running into the main river; usually it would have been only knee deep, but that day it had become a raging torrent, dashing over sharp rocks, and we could not cross it. So our lads looked about and found a tree growing on the bank, one branch of which about ten feet above the ground, stretched over the stream. "We can cross on that," they said. Some of us did, though it was difficult and very slippery. Last of all the Archdeacon crawled over. It was quite a new sight to me—a tall Archdeacon with nothing on, about ten feet above my head, crawling along a slippery bough with somewhat the motion of a large white caterpillar, and with a look of horror on his face. The lesser clergy ought not to see these things. I think he fell off and we caught him; anyhow we went on again.

At last we came near Wakere's village. Here there was a large tree with great flat buttress roots, a natural gong, about a quarter of a mile from the village. You had to beat on this to show you were coming and were friends, otherwise you would be killed before you got to the village—like knocking at the front door at home. So we beat the gong. I said: "Archdeacon, Wakere has heard there is a great dignitary of the Church coming up, and he will be sitting in state to receive us, with some other chiefs. We must make a good impression. I think we ought to put on our clothes."

It was then we found the boy with the Archdeacon's clothes was missing. I dressed hurriedly as I felt the Archdeacon was looking hungrily in my direction—but of course they would not have fitted him. However I lent him my large bath towel. He wrapped it round him rather gloomily and we went on again. When we came to the village and Wakere's house, he was sitting on a kind of dais, with some minor chiefs round him, and as we came in he looked very hard at the Archdeacon. Of course he was expecting something unusual, but even so he seemed surprised. He spoke to me in the native tongue: "Is that an archdeacon?"

"Yes," I said, keeping carefully to the native tongue. "They always dress in a special way." Which of course is true enough.

Wakere seemed quite friendly and promised not to trouble us again. He entertained us well and then we returned to Pamua. But he was not really as friendly as he seemed and afterwards became, for he set an ambush on our way back, men concealed in the bushes at the side of the track, who were to spear us as we went past. But we neither saw nor heard them, and only heard about it afterwards. I don't know why, but it may have been the sudden vision of a tall white archdeacon with a grim, set face, and peculiar costume that daunted the hill men. We got back quite safely—the boy with the Archdeacon's clothes was back already—and never had any more trouble with Wakere, who became one of my friends. Things settled down and the school flourished till there were about seventy boys in it, and I took twelve of them to Norfolk Island when I went there three years later as headmaster after T.C.C.

During the later years of the school many of the boys distinguished themselves. After its amalgamation with Maravovo prep. school, Pamua remained empty for some time, but now there is a girls' school there, with more than a hundred being trained as teachers and nurses, and Pamua flourishes more than ever. The hill villages are gone; there are no cannibals to annoy the girls; and even the crocodiles, which used to come up on the beach when we were there, no longer dare to invade it. St. Michael's Boys' School, Pamua, is only a memory.

CHAPTER FOUR

THE MAKING OF ALL HALLOWS SCHOOL

WHEN the Mission decided to give up its great school at St. Barnabas, Norfolk Island, and establish all its schools in the Islands themselves, Bishop Steward looked about for a good place for a school for older lads in the Solomons. A trader, Joe Dickinson, had leased six hundred acres on the island of Ugi—properly Uki ni masi—and had planted part of it with coconuts. I suggested to the Bishop that this land, called Pawa, would make a good site for a school. Another missionary had already gathered together a number of lads as a nucleus and for two years he carried on a school there, living in the native house Dickinson had built and building some leaf houses for the boys. Then he married and retired from the Mission and the Bishop looked about for someone to carry on, and finally asked me to do so.

The site by the shore, among all the coconuts and close to the boundary where the bush was full of mosquitoes, was an impossible one if the school was to develop. I had to find a new and better site and then build up the school afresh. Between the sea and the nearest hills was a swamp, knee deep in water and full of bullrushes, and the hills beyond that were very steep and covered with thick jungle. I climbed and explored them and found, where Pawa School is now, a hill with a fairly flat top large enough for school buildings. We cleared it of jungle and planted it with sweet potatoes, and I gave a gold sovereign (then fairly common) to each of five schoolboys to build me a small leaf house, twelve feet square, so that I could go and live in it for a month and test the place for mosquitoes. This was the headmaster's house for the next five years.

The test was satisfactory and we gathered the crop of sweet potatoes and began to build on the site. The next thing was to make a road up that very steep hill. Taking a mattock I marked out a line round and up the hill and the boys cut out the road. We then made another road along the edge of the swamp down to the shore. This we made at night by the light of hurricane lanterns and called it the Road of Lanterns. Then we tackled the swamp and cut a deep five-foot drain through the middle of it from the hill to the sea. The boys enjoyed this mudlarking, and when the swamp was drained it made good garden land.

Meanwhile we had been building houses on the hill; first a large dining-hall and then five houses for the boys, and last of all a school chapel. We got ebony from Ysabel for the altar, made a floor of cement mixed with red earth, and seats of palm slats, each boy and master carving one of the legs of the seats. In the end it was a beautiful chapel, large enough for one hundred and fifty boys, but built entirely of native material and so not permanent. The headmaster's house was still the original little leaf house until Bishop Steward at length got a carpenter from New Zealand to build the present one. He was not a missionary and the boys used to gather round to listen to his language when anything annoyed him—it was new to them and very picturesque.

In building the chapel we nearly killed a boy who fell into the five-foot hole just as we were dropping a main post into it—but it would have been according to native custom, for no canoe house used to be built without first putting victims into the holes before dropping in the main posts. It would have been unlucky to omit this precaution.

Those were strenuous years for masters and boys. We made another road at the other end of the hill down to the playing fields, and every year we planted twenty-five acres of sweet potatoes, as well as yams and bananas, as food for the school, now grown to over one hundred boys.

So Pawa School grew and flourished till the Resident Commissioner declared it to be the finest school in the Solomons and began to pay frequent visits. Since the days, fourteen years earlier, when I had the prep school at Pamua, great changes had come to the Islands. The British Government was firmly established, head-hunting and cannibalism had come to an end; you no longer saw marauding canoes stealing along the coast and looking for a victim. British colonialism was doing its excellent work; but still the duties of a headmaster in a Solomon Island boys' school were not quite those of a New Zealand headmaster.

The dress of the boys was simply a blue denim loin-cloth, with a sash which varied in colour according to the house they belonged to. On Sundays they wore a white loin-cloth with a red sash. There were five houses named Gatou, Lion, Pagoa, Gave and Ura (hermit crab, lion, shark, crab, and prawn), and they played against each other every week at cricket or soccer for a cup or a banner. One of the duties of the headmaster was to spend every Saturday morning mending and patching the boys' loin-cloths with the help of a sewing machine. My helper in this was a senior boy (now Canon Parapolo) until my sister came as matron. She was far stricter than I, and would not let the boys dry their things on barbed wire fences. Although her height was only five foot she ruled the boys with a rod of iron, and even six-foot boys trembled when she wagged her finger at them. She was a great gardener and planted flowers and flowering shrubs everywhere; and the hill has never again been as beautiful as she made it then. She took a deep interest in every boy and they were very fond of her. Her knowledge of Mota was not perfect and she startled her cook boy (now Canon Masuraa) one day by calling out to him in an agitated voice that "the bread has risen from the dead" (the words of the Creed, which she remembered), when she only meant that it had come over the tin. Willie looked at the bread gravely without a smile on his face. Melanesians are great gentlemen and will not laugh at one's mistakes—only go and tell them to the other boys with delight—till they know one well.

We were building the school on the lines of Norfolk Island and that meant a model farm as well as a school. We got some Herefords, so the headmaster had to know all about cattle. I knew nothing. I have a memory of my assistant and myself chloroforming a young bull. It was not easy for a man of my size to hold the animal while Jim chloroformed it. The headmaster had to know all about our garden crops, the best manures, green manures and cover crops and rotation of crops; but we steadily improved our gardens till we were getting at least two meals a day, sometimes three, from them for a hundred boys, and our sweet potatoes were giving six tons to the acre. We had drained our swampland and were planting it, but the boys had never seen that done and doubted any good result, so that in answer to a General Knowledge question I set them as to the best ground in which to plant sweet potatoes, one boy wrote: "not in a swamp"—and another more simply: "God knows". The headmaster had to know all about making copra from coconuts, something I had never done. The set of boys who cooked for a week had to make copra the following week. In spite of the then poor price of copra (£6 a ton) we made £200 a year from our nuts and about £50 a year from our pigs (pigs are another thing a headmaster must understand), and in the end a boy at Pawa only cost the Mission from ten to fifteen shillings a year. We were not far from self-supporting.

As for schoolwork, we followed the example of Norfolk Island. We had enough printed in Mota for educational purposes. We had the whole Bible, which the boys knew thoroughly—more than forty of the boys of that time have since been ordained. Once the boys of the first class worked out Q from the Mota version. They got a very good grounding in the Christian Faith, though their arithmetic and general secular knowledge was not half as good as in the later Pawa. In Richard Rudgard I had an incomparably good assistant, and the reputation which the school gained was largely due to him. For the first five or six years my teachers had all been Melanesians. We had a good drum and fife band and a carpenter's shop. Every week we had native dancing, dances by the boys of different islands, and Richard even introduced some English dances. For social service two of the boys went round the Ugi villages every week with medicines and bandages for the sick. My regret is that we did not develop drama as a later headmaster has done. The boys would have loved it.

Being a New Zealander, I had always been a lover of cricket and football, and had played for my school and university. There were fine playing fields which Hodgson had made when he started the school on the flat land below the hills. We had house matches every week, and did not bother about the seasons; we played cricket till all our bats were broken and then soccer till all our balls were burst and we had a new stock of bats. It is true our wicket was not all it should have been and you could not be sure of what a ball would do; seventy was quite a good score for a house eleven. We allowed two and a half hours for two innings on each side, an outright win giving high points. A Melanesian tries to hit every ball for six. In one house match my house made eighty-seven, and as there was only an hour and six minutes left we thought ourselves safe for a win on the first innings; but in that time the other house made two hundred and fifty six in spite of the fact that I was bowling what I pointed out to them were googlies.

Before she came my sister knew nothing of cricket, but she soon became very keen, kept all the boys' averages and was very angry with a boy who had a good average and yet made a duck. She also used to score for us, sitting in our little pavilion. One day a boy hit a ball into a sago palm growing inside the ground. The fielding side appealed in Mota (still Greek to my sister) for lost ball, but I told them to get it, whereupon the whole fielding side rushed across the ground to a small toolshed, seized knives and axes to cut down the palm, and rushed across towards us on the way to the tree. My sister, who had not understood what was said, thought it was a sudden rising. However they ran past us and had the palm down (its stem is too smooth to climb easily but quite soft) before the batsmen had run six.

Our standard was too high for visiting teams and we won almost all our matches. The Bishop said it would do our pride good to have a fall and he would bring a white eleven to humble us. The boys were rather nervous, hearing that the Bishop was a good bat, the Captain a great hitter, and that the engineer had bowled for Essex. But all went well. The Bishop indeed made top score. He made one, and there were three byes. The engineer had bowled Essex, but at seventy-three he was a little stiff and the boys made about a hundred and fifty for two wickets. Our reputation increased.

I was supposed to be an authority on cricket and got enquiries on knotty points from other islands. One came from Gela where the villages then played a lot of cricket. A batsman had hit a ball into the top of a seventy-foot coconut and a fieldsman had climbed up and got the ball. Was the batsman out? There seems to be nothing about coconuts growing on the ground in M.C.C. rules. But there is generally grass on a cricket ground and if it comes off that, not off the ground, is the batsman out? I wrote that a coconut is only a kind of large grass (belonging to the vegetable kingdom and not classed as a "tree" in Melanesian languages—only something with branches is a tree) and so the batsman was not out, a ruling of course open to question.

On another occasion I was umpire in a match on San Cristoval. It was played on hard black sand, quite a good wicket, about twenty feet above the sea, and they had agreed (contrary to the rules) to have no boundaries. A good batsman was in and he hit a loose ball to leg and well out to sea. The fielding side urged me to call lost ball, but I could see the red ball out beyond the breakers, and told the batsmen to run. It should have been a simple thing to get it, but there had been a cyclone and such a surf was breaking on the beach that it seemed doubtful if a fieldsman could get through it. The captain told square leg to go for the ball, but he was a small boy, looked at the surf, and shook his head. It took the whole fielding side to get him in. They threw him in, and the surf tossed him back, and it was only at the third throw that they got him well out; and meanwhile the score mounted. Even then it took time to field the ball; of course every cricketer knows what it is fielding in a heavy sea in the deep. Just as he seized the ball, and tried to throw, a wave would bury him in that rough sea. He got in at last and the batsmen after all had only run fifty-four. Of course the ball was what the rules called "recoverable"; it only needed a little courage on the part of square leg and a little help from the rest of the side. But what if it had become dark and the ball was lost after the batsmen had run about a thousand? A thousand and six runs? We could not well have drawn stumps while a hit was still being run out. It was puzzling for an umpire.

The headmaster's most important work was in the school chapel. It was of good proportions and gave a sense of dignity. It was thatched with sago palm leaf, with a square tower, and as it all weathered to a grey colour it looked like an old stone church. The floor was pale pink from the red earth mixed with the cement; the sides and ends were of woven bamboo in intricate patterns of black and white, worked by a Melanesian artist; the eight-foot ebony altar was very heavy and the reredos beautifully inlaid with mother-of-pearl. My cousin, of Malling Abbey in Kent, sent us a beautiful altar frontal. This chapel was the heart of the school. There was a daily Eucharist before it was quite light. The rest of the boys could lie snug under their blankets for half an hour longer, while those who came to chapel got up in the dark, bathed in the swimming pool, and put on their white loin-cloths, for Melanesians always wear their best if they are to meet the King. I used to take a lantern and go up in the early morning; in the chapel my server had got everything ready and I would see some thirty dim forms in white waiting there on their knees. The chapel and the daily Eucharist are what old Pawa boys seem to remember best. One of them said to me, "It was the daily Eucharist that kept peace in the school." Now a much larger chapel, holding perhaps eight hundred, with a beautiful Lady chapel holding another two hundred, has taken its place.

We had no pulpit and preached from the altar steps, of which there were four broad ones. Now I have always had a horror of spiders, much more than of snakes, and we have very large tarantulas. Sometimes if you were sleeping on a mat in a native house they would fall on you at night with their soft, heavy weight. The small boys used to shoot them with miniature bows and arrows, for they run too fast to be caught. One day while preaching I saw a large one at the end of the step on which I stood. It took a little run towards me and stopped, then a little run and stopped again. I kept one eye on the boys and one on the spider. Suddenly it took a very swift run and climbed up inside my cassock. I managed to finish my sermon and then went hastily into the vestry and shook it out. I would have preferred a snake!

The south-east Solomons are an earthquake region and we had many, usually quite small, but during my nine years at Pawa there were two very big ones, size ten on the Rossi-Forel scale. A small earthquake is nothing much, but when the whole island is shaken as a terrier shakes a rat it is very uncanny. The first big one came just after Evensong when we had heard the lesson about Korah, Dathan and Abiram coming to the mouth of their tents with their wives and little ones and the ground swallowing them up. One of my Melanesian teachers had just returned to his house when the shock came, and he rushed out with his wife and little ones to see Pawa hill open right across at their feet. He said it was too much like the Bible. The boys all went to the shore and I was left alone on the hill, lying on a tarpaulin, and seeing in the moonlight, during the after-shocks, the hills swinging to and fro.

The second earthquake came five years later. After the first tremendous shake of three and a half minutes the hill continued to quiver from time to time for about a week and then came a series of great shakes nearly as big as the first. It was in this earthquake that tidal waves drowned a number of Melanesians. We only had sea waves about five feet high at Pawa but the sea between Ugi and San Cristoval, six miles away, was a wonderful sight, like a tide rip. St. Matthew calls the storm on the lake a *seismos* (earthquake), and seeing the sea that day I felt he might be right and something so unusual might well have troubled the disciples, sailors well used to violent storms on the lake. Galilee was an earthquake country and occasionally experienced very severe ones. Wind came with that violent sea at Ugi, but both wind and sea very quickly subsided.

All Hallows, Pawa, has continued under later headmasters to be a great school, but football and cricket are much less played, and this has resulted in less of these games in the island villages, which I think is a pity. It seemed to me that the boys needed something to replace the excitement of the fighting which was the spice of life to their fathers, and in which many of them had taken part; but later heads of the school were not lovers of these games as I was. Long hours of work largely took their place.

However dancing and drama have been characteristic of the later school, as I shall tell in another chapter. Pawa boys have become clerks for the Government, wireless operators, medical students and some have gone to New Zealand schools, such as Te Aute, St. Stephen's and Ardmore; while others have gone to the Police College at Hawthorn in London; two have taken a University degree in New Zealand. Many are teachers in Solomon Island boarding schools for boys. They all take Pawa traditions with them. King George's School, a Government institution, is now a rival to Pawa; but All Hallows School still has a great name and is doing a great work in the Solomons.

CHAPTER FIVE

LIFE IN AROSI

IN the fifteen years I spent on San Cristoval the greater part of my time was spent in Arosi. I came to know the language as well as my own, wrote a grammar and a dictionary of more than 25,000 words, collected more than a hundred folk tales, translated the four Gospels and Acts and Prayer Book into the language, and became almost a native of Arosi.

Arosi (the accent is on the first syllable, not the second), is the name given to the western part of San Cristoval. These local names are originally given to very small areas, and then come to be extended. Thus Bishop Patteson knew the west end as Bauro from a small area there where he got boys for his school; in the Mission the name came to be given to the whole island. It has nothing to do with the modern Bauro, used for the central part of the island. So with Arosi, which was originally a small area near the village Tawatana, but gradually became used for the whole area from Wango village in the east round to Bia village on the west, the area where only one language is spoken.

I found among the people a curious form of adoption. I had noticed a lad of about eighteen calling a boy of fourteen "grandfather". I felt he could not possibly be his grandson; when I enquired about it I learnt that when someone dies, a young boy is adopted to keep green the memory of the man who has died; he takes his name and status in society. It was very puzzling at first because sometimes he is treated as if he were himself and sometimes as if he were the person whose name he has taken, usually the latter. In this way too an outsider may come into Arosi society by exchanging names with an Arosi man. By taking the name he becomes the person, in Melanesian feeling, because a name is much more important with them than it is with us. There was a case where a zealous District Officer wished to get the names of the people of a village. At that time it was a serious thing for a Melanesian to give a stranger his name, and the people refused, especially as the District Officer insisted that each must give his own name. They were told that unless they did so they must go to gaol. They all went to gaol.

This exchanging of names was a practice followed in most parts of Melanesia. It formed a firm and unbreakable bond between the two who did it, and put each into the status of the other. It was sometimes used to make peace between two villages, or even between two islands, and in this way a name used in one island might find its way into another. Thus Takibaina had become an Arosi name, though baina (big) is not an Arosi word; in Arosi "big" is raha. An Ulawa chief, where paina means "big" had exchanged names with an Arosi chief; and this had led to a firm friendship between the people of Ulawa island and those of western San Cristoval, which still remains. In the same way Arosi people became friends with the people of Santa Ana.

Bishop Patteson, who knew Melanesian customs as few did, had exchanged names with Moto, the chief of Nukapu where he was killed. He was thus Moto to them, and it was for this reason that the people of Nukapu thought it such a terrible crime when one of their own people killed him. The real Moto (if we were Melanesians we should say "Patteson") hunted down and drove off the island the man who had killed the Bishop and broken this bond—had killed, so to speak, their own chief. And in the time of Bishop Patteson a young New Zealander, who afterwards became Archdeacon of Wellington, had visited the island of Gela and exchanged names with a Gela man. To this day the name of that New Zealander is used as a Gela name.

When I lived in Arosi I formed this bond with a young chief named Takibaina. We exchanged names and some of our goods. I became thus an Arosi chief and lived with my own people, so they felt. I lived in the household of Takibaina's younger brother, a married man with three children. I found among other things that Takibaina's debts were now mine, and I learnt a great deal about Melanesian debts, and also about all sorts of Melanesian customs

ST. BARNABAS CHAPEL, NORFOLK ISLAND

"The beauty and awe of this chapel made a deep impression on generations of schoolboys who worshipped in it."

MELANESIAN CHILDREN

"the same in all the islands, and alwa[ys]
something to delight a man's heart."

because of my new status; customs and ways of thought which I never would have heard of at all as an ordinary European living amongst them. Many native problems were brought for me to decide. No one treated me as a foreigner nor has anyone ever since! Coming to Arosi at a later time I was taken to see my friend's grave. They had set up a cross with the words

Charles Fox.
Died June 15, 1919.

We lived in that household the ordinary life of Arosi village people. The house in which we lived was a leaf one, about fifteen feet long and eight feet wide. On the side nearest the sea (always on that side in Arosi houses) was the native stone fireplace on which we cooked our meals. On the other side along the wall were about eight native beds, made of slats of betel palm, each about six inches above the ground, and about a foot apart. The last two were partitioned off for Aitora and his wife and family. Usually there were three or four of us on the other beds. At night we would spread our six-foot loin-cloths over us, not a complete covering, and about four in the morning, when the first cocks crow, a cold wind would come down along the river valley and some or all of us would wake. Someone would feel cold. Between each bed was a small fire, but the fire had long gone out. He would blow on the embers until the house became bright with the blaze, and all of us would cluster round it and have a smoke. At such times they would chat very freely about all sorts of things. Usually I would simply listen, sometimes catching a word I did not know, making a mental note of it, and asking the meaning later in the day. After half an hour or so of this free and unrestrained chat, we would feel warm again, lie down and go to sleep till daylight. These talks, as we smoked together round the fire, were very illuminating about many Melanesian points of view.

At dawn we all rose, bathed in the river, had our morning prayers and then broiled a few green bananas on the embers, which made our breakfast. Then Aitora and his wife and three children and myself would go up to the gardens on the low hills, perhaps

49

two miles away. There we worked till about noon in our garden, when we had a pawpaw or coconut. Then we worked again till about half past three, when we all returned to our house to prepare the main, indeed the only real meal of the day. This was yam soup cooked in a large iron pot, and we all took part in preparing it. my part was usually to get a coconut and husk it with a pointed stick in the ground, upon which one jabbed the nut, and, with a twist very soon acquired, twisted the husk off. Then one split the coconut, took half of it, and sitting on a three legged stool called a *saukai*, scooped out the white; then got salt water and, mixing it with the coconut scrapings, wrung out a rich cream over the soup. To the soup, made always of yams, various relishes were added, such as cabbage, prawns or squids. Then we sat round the pot, each with a half coconut shell as soup spoon, and enjoyed our meal. After evening prayers the evening was spent in talk, people visiting from house to house, or if there were a good moon, dancing, perhaps till midnight, the little children learning the dances by imitating their elders, dancing themselves at the tail end. I found this life kept one very fit and well.

There were of course breaks in the usual routine. Sometimes the children did not go out to the garden, but remained with other children in the village to play their own games. Sometimes all the people of the village would be invited to a feast in another coast village or up in the hills, and we would all go together for two or three days and return with many bowls and packages of puddings. Or we might give a feast ourselves, and then there were long days of preparation, bringing in food from the gardens and filling large wooden bowls with the puddings we made. Some of these bowls were beautifully carved with figures of fish or birds as handles, but those were the old sacrificial bowls, a collection of which I took to Dunedin Museum in New Zealand. The ordinary food bowls were large, black, plain wooden ones; one of them might be two feet deep, a foot broad and as much as three feet long. I have seen forty of these filled with puddings at a feast.

It is an important matter to get the children married, because to a Melanesian marriage is as normal as being born and dying. A celibate life is out of the question. I have written about Arosi marriage in my book *Threshold of the Pacific*, but as I had to do with arranging marriages I may be allowed to repeat part of it here.

If a boy has made a proposal through his father, and the girl's people have rejected it, they are fined a small sum of native money. If a boy has made a proposal and been rejected, or has backed out from it, it is held with some reason that he wants to get married, and any girl may propose to him; if he refuses he will hear some plain talk from his father, who will have to pay a fine.

Generally a boy's parents look about for a wife for him, probably in another village. Then he goes and works for the girl's father for a few months, living in the family and getting to know the girl. He lives with the young men of the village. If the girl likes him she will talk and eat with him; if she cooks some food for him she has accepted him. If she does none of these things he returns home and a fine is paid to his father.

The actual marriage is a very gay affair; most of the people of the boy's village go in the early morning, all dressed in their best, and laughing and shouting, to get the girl. Speeches are made by the best orators. I remember one of them comparing the boy and girl to the two bottom planks of a canoe, very useful joined together, no use apart. The money of the bride price is handed over and there is a great feast, given by the girl's father. The boy and girl eat together, and when, often after a sham fight, she is carried off to the boy's village, he makes a small pudding for her; they eat it together and they are married.

A less formal way of getting married is thought to be rather disgraceful. A man wants his daughter to get married and invites a boy from another village to come and live with him. The boy understands; the man wants him to marry his daughter. He goes and works for the man for two years, accepted as his future son-in-law. Then they are married. No money is given and no feast.

Or, of course, a girl may propose if the boy has tried to get married and been rejected. Perhaps some evening on the beach a girl will come up to him and give him a present, perhaps a woven bag. That is a proposal. They meet secretly and exchange presents.

Someone notices it and tells the boy's father, who goes and talks to the girl's people; everyone helps them, and the girl's people must not refuse. This sort of thing often happens on a night of full moon, when the girl and the lad are on the beach and children playing about. The girl sends the children away and gives the lad something.

A friend of mine named Suniabu told me of his own experience. "As children," he said, "we used to give our things freely to one another. Then my father made a proposal for me, but it was rejected. I didn't realise I had to be more careful about giving or receiving presents. One day I gave a girl a bag; I had no idea of marrying her; but she took it for a proposal and wanted to marry me. I refused. Everyone was very angry with me and my father said I was a disgrace to him. I was ostracized and was so unhappy that I went off on a ship to work on a plantation for a year. Even now that she is married she won't speak to me."

When my friend was a small boy his father gave him a sow. It had a litter of pigs and Suniabu sold these for £20. With the money he bought a daughter (by adoption), a girl about his own age from a village twenty miles away. He was not married, but to Melanesians she was just as truly his daughter as if he had been. About this time Suniabu was much touched by the affection shown him by a lad about his own age, who came and helped him in his garden. He did not realise that his friend was working for his daughter. The friend married her and gave Suniabu £10 as bride price. I said to him, "You lost on that, for you had bought her for £20." "Perhaps I did," said Suniabu, "but then we Melanesians don't compare girls with pigs. He was my friend. If he had only had £5 or £6 I would have given her to him. We are not like white people who think only of money in these things." I apologised for my foolish remark.

Suniabu became the Government chief for the whole of Arosi.

The marriages arranged by parents, with the consent of the boy and girl, were generally happy ones. Of course there were cases of adultery, but there was no divorce until the British Government introduced it. I was on Gela when this happened. The Government sent a policeman through all the villages, including the one where I was staying, telling them that now if they wished to give up their husbands or wives and marry someone else they should go to the District Officer, who, if he thought good, would arrange it. The Gela people were very indignant. It was the new liberal view of the British about marriage, not at all a Melanesian view, at any rate on Gela.

The Arosi people are divided into totem clans, mostly bird clans, and descent is reckoned from the mother, except in the clan of the chiefs, whose totem is the eagle. A chief's son succeeded him, but a boy of another clan could be adopted into this clan, the *Araha* (great) clan, to which I belonged. In every village there were some members of each of the clans, unless it was a very small one. A man knew who belonged to his clan in all the Arosi villages, and if he went about he was sure of getting a welcome from them. The whole structure of their society depended on this clan system, but it is one of the things European influence has been breaking down. Land belonged to the clan, but every member got enough of it to keep himself and his family. Ownership of the land depended on who first brought it into cultivation, and the Arosi people, though they had no knowledge of writing, had very long memories. But there were disputes, and they led to fighting.

There were three main causes of fighting, disputes about land, the fouling of drinking water, and women—the last the most common. Most fighting was very cruel—a village was rushed at dawn and everyone slaughtered; or, more likely, individuals were killed in their gardens or while fishing on the reef, when they were alone and without defence, most often in this case women or children.

There was another sort of fighting. Two villages, Wango and Fagani, the former an Arosi village, the latter outside Arosi, were four miles apart, and hereditary enemies. Half-way between was a fighting ground, and the young men of one village would challenge the young men of the other to come there on a certain day. Then each party would throw spears at the other till someone was wounded, when both parties would return home; much like a Saturday afternoon Rugby match at home.

The usual weapons were spears and clubs, the club called *bwauata* (head-splitter) shaped like a curved paddle of hard black wood, with a groove down it so that it could be used as a shield. I have seen a man holding this in his left hand turn off with the groove a whole shower of spears with wonderful dexterity. A crossbow and a blowpipe were both once used in fighting, but in my time only for birds. Bows and arrows, the usual weapons on Mala, were not used in Arosi. In close fighting men wore large round armlets of shell, very sharp at the edges, with which they cut one another when wrestling. The *kilakila*, a tomahawk on a long five-foot handle, was commonly used, but less in Arosi than elsewhere.

I used to see in earlier days many wounded men in the villages. When at war with another village, a tally was kept of people killed on each side. If one village was three or four in arrears they got hold of a small child from the other and cut off each of its limbs one by one, counting each limb as a life, and so making their tally equal. Living prisoners, brought in bound on a pole like a pig, were put straight on the fire and eaten almost raw.

All the people of Arosi believed that to the west of San Cristoval and far out to sea lay an island of Amazons, all the inhabitants women and very hostile. They had children by the use of banana juice and all were girls. If a canoe should reach it all the men in the canoe would be eaten without mercy.

Perhaps the memory of Arosi feasts, high up on the mountains, is deepest of all. A full moon, brighter than we know it in New Zealand; far below a calm, silver sea; the feathery coconuts in the moonlight; all of us in our ornaments, cowrie shells round knees and foreheads, red and yellow grass armlets; strings of sunblood and moonblood (red and white shell disks); flowers in the hair; all the people gay and excited; the killing of the sacrificial pig (separate food for the Christians) and the rich feast that followed, and the dancing; the singing that went on all night and the speeches of the orators. Each orator would walk back and forth about twelve yards each way, coughing at the turns, talking of old customs, of present needs, perhaps about the Government, and at the end of his oration coming down among us to give each of us a bit of native money for listening to him. And then the walk home, carrying away food to consume at leisure, singing, gossiping, joking, a jolly, laughing crowd of happy people. European influence has been against these feasts, condemning them as a heathen custom, a waste of time, and so on. The people's time would be better given to making copra. But our Church helped to keep them, by and large, turning them in some islands into Christian festivals.

CHAPTER SIX

CUSTOMS OF AROSI

SOME of the Arosi customs I did not see myself, as they had died out; but they were described to me by men who had witnessed them. I used to compare the accounts given by different men in different parts of Arosi; as I did also with the meanings of words I heard before adding them to my dictionary. But most of the feasts, dances, death rites, burial customs, and religious practices were still in full force during my early years in Arosi; some were about to come to an end, such as the Hogasia, the annual lighting of the new fire. I believe after the time I saw it, it never took place again. Sea burial too was becoming very rare. These things are supposed to have been destroyed by missionaries. Some things like cannibalism certainly were, though the British Government also disapproved of this; for the rest I have given my opinion about the passing of these customs in another chapter.

If there was plenty of cruelty there was also plenty of excitement and adventure, plenty of interest in life, plenty of dancing and feasting. Most of the songs and dances were revealed in dreams in which Melanesians had and have a firm belief. They are far more elaborate and dramatic than ours. A man would dream a song or dance and teach it next day to the people. Now they borrow both songs and dances from other islands or from the Fijians or Maoris or even from Europeans. In those days they originated their own.

Some dances were not connected with feasts, but were memories of past times. This was the case with the Mwakomwako dance. Mwako means mud, and the dance is so called because the dancers daubed themselves. The same word in Mota means to adorn; no doubt the original meaning is in Arosi. The dancers wore masks of coconut fibre which completely covered their heads and bodies. Below these they wore dresses as in all other dances, but wrapped round their legs down to their ankles. Some blackened their bodies with mud or whitened them with lime. On their chests they wore a mother-of-pearl crescent moon and above it a necklace of scarlet ferns. The masks, painted black with holes for eyes and nose, were elaborately decorated, and usually they had high conical hats, with long straight hair hanging from them. The dancers were never boys, but usually mature men. They had no clubs, but bows and arrows (not used in San Cristoval in fighting), and they carried old worn-out bags, old decayed bowls full of dead leaves, and wore on their arms and legs bones of cuscus, pigs' jaws, and white leaves. They danced out at dusk, not in the daytime, lifting high their feet and rustling the leaves. This was once the dance of the members of a secret society which had died out before my time, and the dance was now a jest, frightening only the children. Once they had bull roarers. The dance, and the society to which it once belonged, seems akin to the Matambala Society of Gela (now long extinct), the Sukwe of the Banks Islands, and the Dukduk of New Britain. The dancers represented the dead. It is not likely to be seen now. It was done for me once from what the old men remembered.

The remarkable dance called *Airasi* is also now forgotten but was performed forty years ago. It is a dance before a tree. *Airasi* may mean a withered tree, but the dance is also called *Resi*, an old word form meaning "Madam yonder", not modern Arosi. Divination is used to decide which chief is to provide the tree, then he and his party go and cut it down on the third day before the feast, after first sacrificing a pig to the spirits of the dead. They must cut a broad road to it through the forest, then they cut off the top fifteen feet, carry it in very carefully and plant it in a hole in the ground. Round the tree at some distance they make a circle of sprouting coconuts. There is a gateway to the circle, and within it, all round it, as many small squares are marked out as there are villages attending the feast. Wood of all sorts is piled up in these squares, and a pig tied at the corner of each. Then comes a very strange ceremony, the dressing of the tree, like our Christmas tree, with valuable ornaments; but it is dressed as though it were a living chief: low down a chief's anklet round the trunk, higher a chief's leglets, higher still a belt of the finest shell disk money, red and white (sunblood and moonblood); higher still a chief's armlets, and then a mother-of-pearl crescent moon and a white disk representing the sun, such as high chiefs wear on their chests; higher still on his forehead a garland and golden cowries, and last of all a scarlet crown. It is the festal dress of a very high chief, all of the finest workmanship, that the *Airasi* is wearing.

The night before the dance the food is cooked and the people sing all night. Next morning as the sun rises the giver of the feast stands at the gateway and calls, and a group of gaily coloured dancers, their arms painted in bands of red, black, and white, comes out from the forest; and as they dance they move round the circle outside and then within it, dancing all the time, led by singers singing, the early morning sunlight falling on them as they circle round the dressed tree. Then the chief of each village is called up in turn and told to keep the peace, see that good gardens are made, debts are paid and all his people behave well. And finally each chief comes up and is given one of the ornaments on the tree, binding himself to help in making the next *Airasi*, perhaps in six or ten years' time. If any is bold to take the garland and crown of cowries and sunblood (which is very valuable) he binds himself to make a greater *Airasi* than this one. The sacred house near the *Airasi* has wonderful decorations for the occasion, carved figures of birds, fish and crocodiles, with long scarlet grass streamers. It is the gayest dance and feast of all. The *Airasi* is stored away in the sacred house, burnt gradually bit by bit, and the ashes after each burning mixed in the puddings at a feast and eaten with exultation and shouts of triumph. The whole feast is a good deal like the *Walaga* of New Guinea and the *Kole* of the Malay apple tree in the Banks Islands. Bishop Newton of New Guinea has described the former. The latter I saw danced at Mota.

The most important annual ceremony was the lighting of the new fire after all fires on San Cristoval had been extinguished; also in former times, so it is said, at the south end of Guadalcanar and in Ulawa and Ugi islands. It is also a time of prayer for good crops and the welfare of all the people, and a great sacrifice to the creator spirits, or perhaps the creator spirit, a winged serpent with the face of a woman. It is called the *Hoasia*, or, in the rest of the island, the *Hogasia*, i.e. the Sacrifice. It is the great harvest thanksgiving when the crops are nearly mature in February and the first fruits are offered, and the chief ceremonies take place at noon and sunrise. A part is played in it by a sacred tree and a sacred stone; and the centre and source of it is at Haun22 a village outside Arosi; but once every village in Arosi took part in it as the new sacred fire was lit, village by village, after it had first been lit at Haunuu by the high priest of the sun. He held the office by virtue of his descent. His daughter was believed to have a child by the sun, and this child of the sun succeeded his grandfather as high priest. When I saw it the high priest was Haganihinua, a fine courteous old gentleman and a devout follower of the old religion, but one of his associate priests was Sam, the professional murderer, a genial rascal but not at all devout.

At Haunnu were some sacred snakes in a stone enclosure, representing Hatoibari, the creator spirit and winged serpent. The story was once told in a magazine article by a visiting journalist of how I was thrown to these snakes as an offering, but like Daniel's lions they refused to harm me. This was fiction. The snakes were killed by an earthquake which brought the hill upon them.

At Haunuu in 1919 the *Hogasia* lasted three days. On the first day the people brought in two of each sort of garden food. One of each was taken to the east and one to the west and everyone had to touch it, even babies and sick people, and then the food was taken to Haganihinua and hung up in the sacred house. At dawn next day he made a burnt sacrifice of fish and yams, which was carried by his grandson, the next priest of the sun, to a sacred tree. He bit the yam and spat out the bits, saying, "The year is bitter and bad." Next day at noon Haganihinua ordered all fires to be put out, going round himself and pouring water over them, even over hot stones. No one could smoke or chew betel nut till, in every house, the new fire was lit, food was cooked, and all ate a little of it, even the animals.

On the last day trumpets sounded from the sacred banyan on the hill above Haununu, and a canoe was launched with great ceremony and paddled out to sea. The man in the canoe prayed in a resounding voice to the creator spirit for all living things, animals, birds, fishes, and trees, naming each one by one, and as each prayer ended the man in the sacred banyan shouted: Io, Io, as we should say, Amen, Amen. There were prayers that all men might be free from fever and sickness, no rope break in climbing nut trees, none steal from gardens, and all living things thrive and increase; beautiful prayers which I included in our Arosi prayer book. It was very solemn and impressive while the man from the sea prayed and the man from the tree responded, the people standing silent in their ranks.

There followed feast and dancing, while runners went from village to village, carrying the new fire. I have only given a sketch of what was a very elaborate series of ceremonies, followed in each village as the runners reached them, but in much less detail.

These festivals are things of the past. No one now on San Cristoval has seen the dead dancing the *Mwakomwako*; or danced round the decorated tree; or seen the priest of the sun light the new fire, or the man on the sea and he on the land pray for a good year. The *rongo* (dances) are still held, but the life has gone out of them. The feasting and dancing and singing have ceased and vanished like the morning mist when the sun rises; but it is scarcely a morning of clear shining after rain, for instead of dancing the people go to work on the plantations, to make copra, to dig for minerals, and try to follow the new ways of our civilisation which would turn them all into hard-working Englishmen leading a godly, righteous and sober life. No wonder the Arosi people look back with longing to the old days.

CHAPTER SEVEN

AROSI RELIGION

THE man of Arosi believes in a magic which he calls *mena*, the possession of which means success and efficiency. The Americans were thought to be highly endowed with it. The source of all *mena* is in spiritual beings, and when these act in and through material things those too become charged with it, and retain it for some time; the material things are transfused and changed; he calls them "hot", and as the *mena* loses its strength he says they are growing "cold". This is how he feels about the Christian sacraments, above all the bread and wine of the Eucharist.

You may see an Arosi man, skilled (as we say) in heathen magic, set to work to make a storm. He takes a very old shell trumpet, handed down through the generations, fills it with water, sets a dracaena leaf in it, and then blows upon the water. Some would call this childish sympathetic magic; he thinks a storm at sea will follow his little storm in a shell. But while he does these acts he is praying to those dead and gone who once owned the shell; it is their *mena*, not his acts, which will bring the storm; he is telling them dramatically what his wish is.

The prayer of an Arosi man is almost always in dramatic form. Thus when he dances he imitates the action of fishing or hunting to get *mena* for those things, but he no more thinks than we do that merely going through the actions will do it. Or he climbs a tree and breaks the twigs, so that the bones of his enemy, distant though he be, may likewise be broken, but while he does so he is secretly invoking some spirit. His secret prayer is the kernel of the outward act.

Codrington, writing on the belief in *mana* in the Banks Islands, describes it as "a power or influence, not physical, and in a way supernatural; but it shows itself in physical force, or in any kind of power or excellence which a man possesses." The son of an Arosi chief was secluded for two years in a small hut on the shore; no woman came near him; he was made to live a hard life and taught by the old men the traditions of his people. He acquired a great deal of mena, but when he came out to the gay feast that followed he left it all in a small almond nut; no matter how much it might be, all the mena in the world could go into it and the nut would not be full; it has no limitations of space; it is only known to be present by what it does. It may be good or bad power; our word "grace", in its Christian application denoting the action of the Holy Spirit, does not therefore cover its meaning. Some things hold mena better than others; like electricity it is dangerous to approach and touch. Things which hold it best are the bones and hair of the dead; possessions of the dead such as clubs, spears, or stone objects; and certain plants, especially amaranthus and dracaena. Such things impregnated with mena are kept carefully wrapped up and used dramatically to express the wishes of the living to the dead; but there is always secret prayer.

The source of all mena, in the belief of the Arosi priest, is in a supreme being called Agunua, who is in all things and yet distinct from all. But the ordinary Arosi man takes no thought of Agunua, and finds the source of mena in spiritual beings. He believes that each of us has two souls, a good part and a bad part, continually at variance in this life. When a man dies the evil part remains in the world as a source of evil mena; and so an Arosi man often seems to want chiefly to propitiate the dead, really the evil influence and evil mena they leave behind, which impregnates material things or is possessed by living men. The good soul leaps from the leaping rock, Rekenga, at the end of the island and swims through the sea to an island of happiness, where it lives for a time and then bathes in a river called the River of Life, when it becomes united with Agunua, without losing its own identity. There was no hell according to Arosi belief. The object of the ordinary man's religion was to receive and use helpful mena, and to avoid or overcome harmful mena, either that purposely directed against him, or what he came in contact with by accident. To achieve this end he prayed continually, in the dramatic form of an acted prayer. Of course many of them, like many Christians, were content with the outward act. Europeans laughed at Arosi religion, and traders told them that it was all nonsense and "debbildebbil". I did not agree with that opinion.

When a man died the separation of the evil soul of him from the good one was not completed till the fourth day, and there were all sorts of things to be done. People crowded into the house where the man was dying. If he were a chief, as soon as he died the people rushed about shouting, shamfighting, and exulting, lest the news of it should first be known in Gath. The body was treated in different ways according to the mode of burial the dead man had asked for, but usually it was wrapped in mats, and always the thumbs and the big toes tied together. There were more than twenty ways of disposing of the body: in a grave lying down, sitting, or standing; on a tree platform (generally a banyan); in a cave; in a wooden carved container, often shaped like a fish; in a hollow tree; if a child, in the house itself; if a chief in a chamber on a truncated pyramid. Chiefs who were embalmed were taken to a cave in the mountains and they are said to be there to this day, but no one seems to know where. Some corpses were cremated and some buried in the sea.

When a man dies some men come into the house and fish with long fishing rods for the evil souls of dead men, who come crowding into the house at a death. The bait is dracaena leaves. The men feel the rods bend and catch many evil souls (adaro), and carry them away to throw into the sea. The night of the burial people gather in the house and tell many death stories, told only at this time. The teller of the tales pauses from time to time and all sing, and call aloud the name of the dead, and outside he answers and calls the names of all those who will die that year. At Pawa when a boy died the schoolboys would hold mirrors towards the cemetery, and declare they could see the ghost of the dead boy in the mirrors. At sunset after a death a man called *Ango i rae* goes to the grave and shouts and the dead are said to answer with thunder.

And then the famous death song, the *Peko*, is sung; very old because the words are an archaic form of Arosi, and inexpressibly sad, beginning *Peko iata mai Kaiko* (Ancestor, my mother is coming).

Cremation seemed to be used chiefly with enemies slain in war. A great pile of firewood was set up and the corpse of the dead man was set upon it, and the firewood set alight at night. In the dark the flames often seemed to be pouring out of the mouth of the dead man. Sea burial was dying out, but you could still go into some quiet, sheltered cove, and there see below you through the clear green water the dead sitting or standing on the yellow coral sand at the bottom of the little bay, swaying gently to and fro with the motion of the sea. Sharks did not trouble them. If they wished to stand, their feet were weighted, if to sit, the weights were fastened round their loins. A man in a canoe paddled out towing a canoe with the corpse in it. He then dived down and fixed the corpse. In case the evil soul should follow him, he paddled his canoe rapidly in circles to make the *adaro* giddy. Then when he got to the shore he took other precautions. He took half from each of two coconuts, so that putting these together a whole nut was formed, but with its two halves not quite fitting together. The evil soul following would see this, and with its instinct for tidiness, stoop and try to make the two halves fit, turning them round and round in its annoyance, so that the living man had time to get well away. It seems childish, and such things generally greatly amuse Europeans, who never, of course, do childish things.

The *heo* on which chiefs were buried were pyramids originally of undressed blocks of stone, going up in steps to a height of about thirty feet, with a large flat top. In my time only two or three of the stone *heo* remained; they were chiefly natural mounds which had taken the place of the stone *heo*. On the flat top was a dolmen, two slabs of stone with a third slab laid across them; this was the altar of sacrifice. Beside it was a roughly carved stone figure representing the dead chief and painted red. At the opposite end of the

Here dancing and drama help to replace the fighting which was the spice of life to their fathers.

ALL HALLOWS SCHOOL, PAWA
"the finest in the Solomons."

Much of our travelling has to be done in small ships such as this mission launch.

Ini Kopuria, founder of the Melanesian Brotherhood.

Commissioning of brothers. "T[ ] went up two by two into the [ ] villages."

flat top of the pyramid was a shaft leading down into a burial chamber, where the corpse of the chief was laid on a bed. Every day a man called the Keeper of the Dead carried the corpse to running water, and there daily he stood with the corpse on his shoulders while water was poured over it, and gradually all the flesh came away. The bones were then carefully preserved in a carved wooden figure of a shark. The Keeper of the Dead had a bag over his head and shoulders while doing his unpleasant work, and was well paid.

Before the corpse of the chief was placed on the *heo* it was laid in a canoe, called the Canoe of the Dead (also the Canoe of the Heavens), which was raised on trestles ten or twelve feet high, and everyone had to walk underneath. The chief's soul was believed to voyage to the sun. When he died, a victim was always killed, if possible some one at a distance, if not one of the boys of the place.

Some Arosi men were were-sharks, who had exchanged souls with sharks. Such men would go down to the shark rock and call their familiars by name, and the shark would then be sent to kill some enemy fishing in a one-man canoe. It would overturn the canoe and bring the man to its master at the shark rock. The man was always in a dazed condition not able to remember who he was, and weak and helpless. The shark man usually killed him. The son of a were-shark would become one also. His father took the boy, probably to the shark-rock, crooked his left arm like a shark's fin and hugged him. Then a shark was called up and the boy and shark exchanged names and souls, or were both given the same name. If the child died the shark died. Once from my boat we shot one of these sacred sharks and the shark man died at the same time in a village further along the coast. I was accused of murder. Even when shark boys went fifteen hundred miles away to the Mission school at Norfolk Island their sharks were said to follow them and meet them at the rocks there, ready to obey their master's commands.

These are only odds and ends of Arosi customs and beliefs. No Arosi man was a materialist. But now he has met with Europeans, evidently with more *mena* than he has; and most of those he meets with are materialists who scorn his beliefs, or else are Christians who tell him his beliefs are childish, yet who themselves belong to different Christian communions, the members of each thinking the others quite wrong and not to be followed. What is he to think? The people's old beliefs are deep in their minds, and many have said, "Let us return to our own beliefs and customs and way of life, which are better for us than the white man's ways." This was good ground in which to sow the seeds of "Marching Rule", the movement which followed the upheaval of all their ideas in the Japanese war, a nationalist movement for self-government and the expulsion of all Europeans.

CHAPTER EIGHT

A MELANESIAN BROTHERHOOD

THE *Retatasiu*, which means "Company of Brothers", is a Melanesian Brotherhood, of which I was a member for eleven years, the only white man among more than a hundred Melanesians. It began more than thirty years ago with a young man named Ini Kopuria, born at Maravovo in Guadalcanar and named after a great Anglo Saxon Christian king who ruled in my native Dorset long ago. He went to Pamua about the time I left that school, but he was still there when I returned to San Cristoval and had my headquarters quite close to them. I did not see very much of him then. He was, I remember, a very dark little boy, very full of fun and very keen in school.

At that time I was wondering how to get into touch with the hill villages, for I had no teachers to send up into the hills. To meet this difficulty I formed a small Brotherhood of young Melanesian lads who had finished school at Norfolk Island. It was called St. Aidan's Brotherhood and they promised to take no pay, to remain unmarried and to go wherever they were sent, for as long as they remained in the Brotherhood. They went up two by two into the hill villages and after two months of this returned to our headquarters for a month of teaching and then went off again to the hills. The leader was Ellison Kokou from Ini's village of Maravovo, a lad of very great promise who died only a few years later; otherwise I am sure he would have become an outstanding priest. This Brotherhood did not last very long, but Ini, then at school close by and a friend of Ellison, may have kept the memory in mind when he came to found his own greater Brotherhood twelve years later.

After Pamua, Ini went on to the school at Norfolk Island, where he stayed for some years and made his mark as a schoolboy. The story is told of him there of how he decided to keep Lent. When asked a question in class he was silent and passed up to his teacher a paper on which he had written, "I have decided to fast in Lent by not speaking to anyone. Please don't ask me any questions in school." Knowing Ini I feel this was a severe form of fasting. He happened to be coming home in the Mission ship when a cyclone struck her in the Banks Group and Captain Burgess brought her safely through those islands, full of reefs, on a very black and wild night. Ini was with the other boys and playing the fool as he loved to do. A missionary came to the boys and found Ini laughing. "Ini! Ini!" he cried, "stop laughing! Don't you know we are all going to die?" It took more than a cyclone to keep Ini serious.

Ini returned to his home but did not become a village teacher as he was supposed to do. It seemed to him too tame a life. He became a native policeman and by and by a sergeant under a District Officer who thought very highly of him. But after a few years of this he became seriously ill, and he told me he had then a vision of our Lord telling him he was not doing the work he was meant to do. That was all. He went home and spent some time with Arthur Hopkins, then in charge of the Mission College at Maravovo, to think out his next step.

It was when he was with Hopkins, and partly through Hopkins, that the idea of a Brotherhood came to him. He went to Bishop Steward and told him he wanted to found a company of Brothers who would take the Christian Faith to every village where he had gone as a policeman to get prisoners. The Bishop was the right man to go to. A few years before his consecration he himself had wished to form a Brotherhood of priests to go and live in the centre of Mala, the wildest island in the Solomons, and had asked me if I would be one of them. Together he and Ini worked out the rules of the new Brotherhood and they gave it the name *Retatasiu*. I was then headmaster of All Hallows, Pawa, and Ini came to me and asked if he might speak to the boys. Several of the senior boys joined him; two of these were Dudley Bale and Moffat Ohigita, both of Ysabel, which has sent out so many missionaries. Both later became priests. The Brotherhood began, with seven Brothers, when Ini took a lifelong vow on his own land at Tambalia, given by him to the Brotherhood. The others took a vow for one year.

The rules were very simple and good. The first gave the aim of the Brotherhood, which was to take the Christian faith to the heathen, first those of Guadalcanar and then to the rest of Melanesia, and then—as Ini always said—to New Guinea, Indonesia, and beyond. The Brothers were to go two by two always, none was ever to go by himself. They were to be organised in Households, not more than twelve in a Household, with a *Moemera* (elder brother) at the head of each, and Ini himself at the head of the whole Brotherhood. The Bishop was to be the Father of the Brotherhood and his decisions were to be final if a dispute arose. The whole Brotherhood was to meet once a year at their headquarters on S. Simon's and S. Jude's Day, the day Ini took his vow. Each Brother took a vow not to marry, not to take any pay, and not to disobey those over him. This vow was for one year and could be renewed at the annual meeting. Most remained in the Brotherhood for five or six years, but one at least (besides Ini), remained in it for the rest of his life. The Brothers, of course, were bareheaded and barefoot; their dress was a black loin-cloth and a white sash; on Sundays and saints' days they wore a white loin-cloth and black sash; and on great occasions, a white singlet. This was my own dress for eleven years. It is the ordinary dress of Melanesians, and the best for that climate.

One rule of the Brotherhood was that no Brother must criticise another to anyone else. On the other hand if he saw anything wrong in the conduct of another Brother he must not brood over it silently but must speak about it at the annual meeting. Then the Brother accused replied, and then all discussed it freely; it soon became clear who was in the wrong and he apologised. Ini always began with the Brother who had joined last and asked each in turn if he had anything of this sort to tell us. Later each Household held such a meeting every week and this rule led to our working together with good feeling and friendliness to each other.

Ini was without doubt our leader. He was a short, thick-set man, very strong, very dark and with a merry face. I never met anyone with such a zest for life. Whatever he did he did with all his might.

Technically he was not a good footballer, but he played with such energy and fire that it was good to have him in the team. In everything he did he was the same. He was also wise and full of common sense; he had very good judgment as to what was practicable and what was not. He was very patient with Brothers who were giving trouble and always seemed to see their point of view. No one disputed his leadership and all trusted him. His relationship with the Bishop was that of a son to a father and they were very fond of one another. I remember once at an ordination we all came out of the church and stood in two ranks for the Bishop to pass through; Ini, as the Bishop passed by him, bowed very low and the Bishop paused and turned and bowed low to Ini—a beautiful thing to see. He might be troubled sometimes, yet he was always rejoicing.

Such was the man under whom I served, one of the two ablest Melanesians I have known. I had better tell the end of his story. For twenty years he worked in the Brotherhood. Then came the war, with all its confusion and unsettlement. Ini was in the thick of it. After an affair with a woman he went out of the Brotherhood, absolved by the Bishop from his vow; very unhappy, he died soon afterwards—a clouded evening after a sunny day, but peace at the end. I cannot imagine such intense vitality can end with death. He was a little like St. Peter, impetuous, sometimes self-confident, but like St. Peter always ready to acknowledge a mistake, and like St. Peter he could repent deeply.

There was nothing small about him. I never knew him to lie and I never knew him to fail a friend.

When I joined the *Retatasiu* I was for a year under Brother Dan, the Head of the Tambalia Household. He had been one of my schoolboys at Pawa so our positions were reversed. He was a good Head, and after he left the Brotherhood became one of our best priests. A number of Brothers after leaving us became priests, it proved a training ground for ordination. Tambalia was where we trained our novices and that was my work for some years.

The annual meeting, when all the Households came in and we all met one another again and had a week together, was something we all looked forward to. Every Head of a Household presented a report of the work each Household had done during the year, and we all discussed it, praising or blaming them for their work. One year we had a Household working at Tulagi, the capital, visiting the hospital and gaol and taking prayers with the crews of the many small ships that gathered there. We had heard that the Brothers had not been visiting the gaol and several got up and taxed them with this. The Head of the Tulagi Household rose to reply and pretended to be very much upset. "Brothers," he said, "you are quite right—we have not been visiting the prisoners in the gaol." He paused and hung his head, then said quickly, "You see we are only allowed to visit prisoners of our own church, and unfortunately there have been no Anglicans in gaol this year, but next year we are hoping there will be plenty of them."

On the last day of the annual meeting the Brothers renewed their vows and the novices were received into the Brotherhood. They all gathered on a lawn in front of a twelve-foot Celtic cross which stood where Ini had made his vow. The Bishop in cope and mitre stood in front of the cross and first the novices made the threefold vow, put on the Brotherhood dress and knelt while the Bishop laid hands on them. Then each of the ten or twelve Households came up and renewed their vows in a body. Each Head of a Household carried a candle which the Bishop lit saying, "Let your light so shine before men that they may see your good works and glorify your Father in Heaven." When all had returned to their places the whole company of perhaps a hundred and twenty Brothers knelt while the Bishop blessed them and sent them out to another year's work. To see this company of more than a hundred young Melanesian missionaries kneeling there in white loin-cloths, their lights burning, for the Bishop to bless them, is something I can never forget. I was one of them.

The Households went out to different islands, some to Guadalcanar, some to Mala, some to Santa Cruz, some to one of the Polynesian islands, some to New Britain; and lately some have gone to New Guinea. While I was a Brother I visited all these places except the last.

There is a story told of the earliest Brothers who worked on Guadalcanar. It was told me by Brother Dudley, one of the first

Brothers, and was his own experience. He and Brother Moffat had gone up into the mountains, which are 8,000 feet high. They climbed a steep cliff, dragging themselves up by creepers, and at the top they found a heathen village, where they were well received by the chief, but next morning things were different. The chief told them the village priest had come to him in the night and said to him, "Drive them out. I have seen a third brother with them whose face shines and terrifies me. Let us have nothing to do with them." So out they were driven.

Many Brothers worked on Mala, where in my time there were over fifty thousand heathen. Two of the Brothers went up into the hills, where the people were still wild, and work was very difficult and dangerous; where often Brothers would have to go three or four days without food and were told to sleep in pigsties; or were still more roughly treated. These two came to a hill village in the middle of the day when all the people were out in their gardens; but they went into one of the houses, where they found a lad crippled with terrible tropical ulcers, unable to walk and lying on a mat. His father, who was the village chief, returned, and seeing the shadows of strangers on the threshold, rushed in to spear them. The lad stopped him and said they were friends, and the Brothers asked him if they might take his son to their Household on the shore and heal him. The father said he had tried everything and there was no hope, nor could they get him down to the shore. But in spite of his stinking sores they carried him down pickaback, taking turns, over the twelve miles of steep hills, kept him there for a month or more till his sores were healed, and then took him home to his father, who asked for a Christian teacher. They called this "opening" a heathen village, and that is one way to do it.

In 1900 the Bishop estimated the population of Santa Cruz to be between thirty and forty thousand. I think it must have been much less. At any rate it went steadily down and they always refused to have Mission schools. I think in 1915 the number had dropped to less than ten thousand and was going down rapidly with all the villages still heathen. It was very depressing to go there and see the people dying out. A Mission priest, George West, did some good work, but the real change came when the Brothers went and began their schools. I went there later and was amazed to see the change—clean houses, healthy people, in many Christian villages. The people seemed happy and full of life. It was a different island from the Santa Cruz of twenty years earlier. They now have a Santa Cruzian priest of their own.

A change of the same sort came to Lord Howe Island, which has a Polynesian speaking people. In 1860 the population was said to be fifteen thousand, but malaria was introduced by a trader, and gradually the numbers went down till only two hundred and fifty remained, although they are a fine race. Methodist missionaries went there but did not stay long and no one was baptised. When it seemed that soon there would be no one left I took a Household of Brothers there who settled down and worked well. The population has gone up, and the last time I was there it was eight hundred and fifty and increasing. The Japanese landed there in the war, but did nothing except go into the church and burn the people's books.

Households of Brothers went to New Britain. I was on board the Mission ship as we steamed along the south coast of that big island, looking for a place where we could settle the Brothers among a people who were all heathen. We eventually anchored off a village on a small island where the people seemed friendly and agreed to let the Brothers stay and teach them. The two we put down had only enough personal luggage to fill their two haversacks—beyond that nothing at all except a blackboard and some chalk. As I rowed off to the ship from the shore I saw two lonely figures, standing on the beach, eight hundred miles from their own homes, among a people of whose customs and language they knew nothing, who might easily kill them or starve them when we were gone, for they had not the prestige of white men. I thought them brave lads, each about eighteen years old. In a year's time we came back. The two Brothers were standing waiting on the shore, but with them now were twenty people they had prepared for baptism. Later I think there were three hundred Christians there from that small beginning. One of those two Brothers became in later years a priest.

A vivid memory is a baptism at Sagsag at the western end of New

Britain near Cape Gloucester. Ini had been there with some of the Brothers and prepared these people. Up to that time there were only about twenty Christians but that day we baptised more than two hundred. There was a beautiful river coming down from the mountains, running over a gravel bed, clear cold water, waist deep in the middle; on the west side was a high grassy bank, where we set the Bishop's chair, and there he sat in cope and mitre with twenty Christians round him. The people to be baptised gathered on the other side, with a crowd of heathen who had come to see. Ini and I stood in the middle of the river, and streams of people came to us to be baptised. Then they passed over to the Christian side, took off the ragged loin-cloths they had been wearing, and put on clean white ones, and joined the Christians standing round the Bishop. It took some three hours; I know my legs were numb with the cold water. Then we formed a long procession and went up the hill to the Church, far too small to hold us all. The procession, I remember, was so long that we were singing different verses of a hymn in different parts of it, but it was a joyful crowd, and a baptism I shall always remember. We always baptise adults in a river.

And now Ini's dream has come true and these Melanesian Brothers have gone out beyond the bounds of Melanesia into New Guinea, as he always hoped they would. Brother Andrew, the Head of the whole Brotherhood, has taken nine others with him and gone up into the New Guinea highlands five thousand feet above the sea, where there are no Christians but thousands of heathen, who know nothing of our Christian Faith. Before they left by aeroplane I had the privilege of teaching them for three months. We read together, chiefly in the Mota language, which they all speak, though some now speak English, of Antony, Benedict and Francis; of Ignatius, Polycarp, Cyprian and Augustine; of the early missionaries to England and of our own missionaries to Melanesia. We studied the life and words of our Lord; the sacraments of the Church, the Lord's Prayer and the Ten Commandments. They spent a good deal of time practising singing. We spent an hour together daily in the chapel. And then at the Brothers' annual meeting the Bishop sent them out with his blessing to work under Bishop Hand of New Guinea. They make good missionaries, living the life of the people to whom they go. After six months they wrote that more than a thousand people were coming to their teaching and some five hundred children to school. Brother Andrew, who led them, had been twenty years in the Brotherhood, and is a disciple of Ini.

There were a number of young men who wanted to join the Brotherhood but did not feel they had enough learning to go to the heathen as evangelists. The Bishop had bought the Brothers a piece of land on Ugi which included an island called Bio four miles off the coast, and this had been partly planted with coconuts by Messrs. Levers. Here they could be self-supporting by making copra, especially on Bio island, and on the land on Ugi they began a school for boys from heathen villages. It was suggested that men who wanted to join the Brothers but were not qualified to be evangelists might work the coconut plantation to help the Brotherhood. This was done. They were received into the Brotherhood, said the Brothers' offices daily, and made copra. We called them our Copra Brothers.

There was more than one weakness in the work of the Brothers. For instance, one rule forbade them to remain more than three months in a heathen village where they had begun a Christian school. It was to be handed over to a Church teacher. But the Church was seldom ready with a teacher, and when the Brothers left the village it either became heathen again or more likely accepted a teacher from some other Christian communion, Roman Catholic or South Sea Evangelical Mission. This happened in at least thirty cases. The villages remained Christian but not of our Church, though we rejoiced at their accepting the Christian faith.

A more serious weakness, which became acute after the war, was the difficulty in finding Brothers good enough for training the novices. When Bishop Steward retired, he wrote an open letter to the Melanesian Church saying that he put his trust in Pawa School to strengthen and uphold the Brotherhood. He hoped lads of eighteen or so when they left school, before they settled down and married, would become Brothers for several years. But Pawa became an English-speaking school and boys who finished their schooling there were able to find well paid work with the Government, and few of them cared to become a Brother with no pay. Pawa failed the Brotherhood. This meant also that it became hard to find leaders for the Households, for there also the Bishop had put his trust in Pawa. Many young men wanted to join the Brothers, but they were men with little or no education and no training in leadership.

The white staff was critical of the Brothers—unjustly so, so the Melanesians thought. They thought young Melanesians joined just for the glamour of it, and it was true that there was not enough stress on real vocation for the Brotherhood life, and lads were joining for only one or two years and leaving again because they had never had any real calling.

The one purpose of the Brotherhood, the taking of the Christian faith to the heathen, was not kept in view either; Brothers were asked by the authorities to do all sorts of odd jobs: rebuilding a church, helping to move a school, acting as caretakers of a Mission station. One leading priest of the Mission went so far as to say that they were merely looked upon as cheap labour. They were not regarded as members of a Religious Order—except by the Melanesians, who have always held the Brothers in the highest honour and treated them almost with reverence; but then they know how hard a Brother's life really is, what real sacrifices he makes, and what a deep and true motive for becoming a Brother many of them have. I have always thought of missionaries as an order of their own in the Catholic Church, parallel with the order of the clergy who build up and rule a Christian church once established; and of equal honour. The church is not a number of people who happen to agree in their opinions on religious matters, but a divine society founded by the greatest of all missionaries, the Son of God, and receiving what He taught. Then He sent others—apostles, missionaries, call them what you will, to pass on this teaching; and those who hear, pass it on again. Thus the Church is apostolic or missionary through and through. When it ceases to be so it dies. Wherever it is planted we have—in time—first apostles, or missionaries, prophets and evangelists, and then after the church is firmly established, pastors, teachers, governments and so on. The two kinds of work are distinct. No doubt some missionaries are already priests. This is needed so that they may receive the sacraments themselves and as soon as there are some baptised Christians in the newly founded church those also may receive them. But their function as missionaries is primary and as priests secondary. So I have held a missionary Brother in as high honour as I hold a priest of the Church, though most people hold him to be of no more importance than a village teacher.

Ini was a great organiser. He wanted the Brotherhood to rest solidly on the Melanesian Church, not on white people. So he established another Order, the Order of Companions of the Brothers, to help the Brothers, the missionaries of the Melanesian Church, with prayers and alms. The idea was all his own, and he himself wrote the rules which have been printed in different island languages. The Companions enter the Order by renewing their baptismal vow publicly in church. They are both men and women, and are organised into Households like the Brothers, each of eight to twelve members. In a large village there might be two or three Households. Each Household has its Leader and each district a Leader of the whole district; and the Companions of each district meet together once a year on St. James' day, under the Leader, to discuss their affairs. Brothers visit them from time to time to tell them about their work, and some of the leaders of the Companions go to the Brothers' annual meeting and pass on what they hear. Like the Brothers themselves the Companions need good leaders. It is a movement with great possibilities if it can get the leaders it needs, and support from the clergy.

The Companions in a village meet together every Friday, one week to pray for the work of the Brothers and the second week to pray for the Church in their own village. But Ini said you would not get people to support missionaries unless they were red-hot Christians themselves, so it was a rule of the Companions that each must do something practical for his own village—clean the church, keep in order the church grounds, serve at the Eucharist, collect firewood for the old people who could not do it for themselves, visit the sick.

Some of the Melanesian priests looked askance at the Order of Companions, thinking the Companions would consider themselves more holy than others. This of course is a danger. But more than two thousand Melanesians have become Companions and they have been of immense help to the Brothers. They used to welcome and help us everywhere, so that wherever we went we could rely on them. When the ten Brothers were going to New Guinea they went first for ten days preaching in Gela villages, and the people—very poor people—gave them £60 for their work.

When I was a Brother I once visited a village on Gela and received as always a great welcome from the Companions there. I slept there, lying on a mat by the leaf wall of the house, and in the night a centipede crept down the wall and bit me on the eye. Now the bite of a centipede is very painful for fourteen hours or so. The Companions were anxious about me when my feet and hands grew cold. They heated leaves and rubbed my feet with them, but I suppose they thought I was not responding as I ought, so they went out, dressed in white and came in and read the commendatory prayer for the dying. This was too much. I got up and walked home.

What results has the Brotherhood to show? It has converted a fair number of heathen people. An anthropologist who went to work on Tikopia told me that the real change on that island from heathenism to Christianity came when a Household of Brothers went there. That was certainly true of Santa Cruz. But I think perhaps the chief result has been to make the Melanesian Church more missionary-hearted than it was before. It is so easy for a church to be content with its own Christian life of prayer and sacraments and to care little about making the whole world Christian, in fact to neglect our Lord's last command. Also the Brotherhood has been a seed-bed for the Christian ministry; many Brothers have gone on to ordination. I could wish some of these had remained in the Brotherhood.

In the war the Brothers had a difficult time. Their headquarters at Tambalia were invaded by the Japanese, their church burnt to the ground, and their houses destroyed, their books burnt, their gold paten and chalice (the gift of their first Father, Bishop Steward) carried off. Some of them had a very narrow escape at Tambalia. They were coming up the bank of the river which runs through it when they came on a party of Japanese with their rifles stacked against a tree. The Japanese rushed to seize the rifles and the Brothers fled. One jumped into a pool of the river and feigned to be dead. After a glance at him the Japanese ran after the other three, who made for the sea. As they swam out the Japanese on the shore stood firing at them. One was shot and killed. Another had a ball pass over his head, making a neat hollow as it shaved a line through his hair. But the two survivors swam four or five miles down the coast, landed and got back safely to Tambalia.

After the war the Brothers were much reduced in number. Ini was gone and they had no good leaders. Now there are seventy of them, and in Brother Andrew they have a man of outstanding personality, who is also a devout Christian, as their Head. Some day there may spring from this Brotherhood a Teaching Brotherhood, not to replace the present order, but to supplement its work and consolidate it. My own years in the Brotherhood were some of my happiest years in Melanesia. It is impossible to convey in words the friendliness, and the fun among the Brothers; or the goodwill and comradeship towards them of all Melanesians, Christians of all sorts and heathen as well. They all had a special place in their hearts for the Brothers of Melanesia.

CHAPTER NINE

TRAVEL IN THE SOLOMONS

THE diocese of Melanesia had always been a sea diocese and during the years much of my time was spent on the Mission ships, ketches and whaleboats. Bishop Patteson's ship was the *Southern Cross* and there have been six others since then, all with the same name. The first of the name was wrecked at the mouth of a river north of Auckland. There was no missionary on board when the ship ran ashore at night. The ship's company climbed the mast and sang hymns till daylight when they found she was on the sand in shallow water and they could have waded ashore at any time. The cook on this ship afterwards became Chancellor of the British Exchequer and used to tell stories of his days in Melanesia. In vain I have tried to encourage later cooks with this example; they all preferred to remain cooks.

The first ship of that name in which I travelled was *Southern Cross IV*, I think of about 250 tons with an auxiliary engine which the previous ships did not have. But she was not a good ship. There were no cabins, but bunks round the long and narrow saloon, with very little room between the table and the bunks. She was the first ship to carry a woman missionary, but her quarters were worse than ours, for to get to them you opened a trapdoor in the 'tween decks and went down into the dark; the Melanesians objected to her walking on the upper deck too, because there she would have been above them, and in those days in Melanesia it was thought wrong for a woman to be in a higher place than a man.

We had very bad weather during my first voyage and spent most of our time working the pumps. When the storm subsided and calm weather came it was wonderful to see the colour of the water changing to a lovely blue, almost a washing blue colour, and we felt ourselves in a new world. Every morning we all went on deck and were hosed down. We had a visiting priest on board and when he went to bed in his bunk he put his false teeth in a glass on the sideboard by the door of the saloon. A missionary getting up in the middle of the night for a drink of water felt something rattle in the glass and deftly pitched it overboard, and had his drink. It took a lot of explaining to our visitor.

Southern Cross V was our largest (500 tons) and our most famous ship, for she served us for about thirty years and in that long career had only two captains, Capt. Wm. Sinker and Capt. Burgess. The former was the son of my father's Hebrew tutor at Cambridge and he was both an excellent captain and a good churchman. He was full of fun and had a lively wit, but had no time for pretentiousness or people who thought themselves superior, and he liked to pull the leg of a new missionary. He was short and stout and once as we were coming into Auckland harbour the Bishop had a bet with him that he could not climb through the saloon porthole, which was rather a large one. Sinker was game for anything and managed to wriggle his head and shoulders through, but there he stuck fast; nothing he could do could get him either through or back again. Presently we should be at the wharf and the captain giving berthing orders in this unusual position. However by pulling his shirt off and oiling him we got him back in time. He wrote an account of his first voyage to the islands called *By Reef and Shoal*, which is a small classic and full of humour. He was the first to have a Melanesian crew, put them into uniform and train them.

A voyage with him that I remember was when we ran into a cyclone. What made it dangerous was that we were trying to carry enough coal to last the whole voyage and had twenty tons of it on deck. In the cyclone with the huge sea that was running this got into the scuppers and blocked them and the water was up to the bulwarks. The women's cabin was aft. We had on board Miss K., one of the first women missionaries to work on Gela, and the water made it impossible to open the door of her cabin; we had to feed her through the skylight, until we had managed to throw all the coal overboard and clear out the scuppers. We lost the whole twenty tons. From the saloon, two alleyways led aft with cabins opening from them. Off

F

the port alley were two cabins and a mailroom. I was sharing one of the cabins with another passenger, he in the lower bunk. About 2 a.m. at the height of the cyclone a huge wave burst in the iron door forward of the saloon and filled it up about level with the tables and poured down our alleyway and into the mailroom and our cabin. There was a newcomer sleeping on the floor of the mailroom, very miserable and frightened, who for some days had been calling "Steward! Steward!" at frequent intervals, though there was no voice nor any that answered. With the coming of this water he floated about, his cries increasing. I said to my companion as the water poured into our cabin, "Drummond, the ship is going down, we had better get up". I suppose I was determined to keep cool, for I sat up and carefully put on a pair of dry socks before stepping down into two feet of water. Drummond and I waded into the saloon. The Bishop was not on board, but his three small children were, in the charge of a nurse. When we reached the saloon we could see by the dim light of an oil lamp the nurse and two elder children standing on the settee just out of reach of the water, while the baby in the cradle sailed back and forth across the saloon like another Moses, as fresh waves poured in. However we managed to get the iron door shut again, and slowly and gradually baled the water out aft down our alleyway. At the height of the storm a man was washed off at the bow while wearing his oilskin and sea boots; as he passed amidships the mate threw him a rope and pulled him on board; he was very excited and kept repeating, "I've lost my sea boots!" and so he had. When I went on the bridge I was amazed at the awesome sight of the waves looking like mountains in all directions.

In all the hundred years of the Mission two of our ships have been wrecked, *Southern Cross I* and *Southern Cross VI*. The latter was wrecked in the New Hebrides on her first voyage, and the two members of the Melanesian Brotherhood on board showed great bravery; and the mate also, when the ship sank, made a long voyage in a whaleboat from Aneityum to Vila to get help for the stranded ship's company. On that occasion, too, there was no missionary on board. Five missionaries have been drowned. George West, when his launch was driven ashore in a storm on Utupua, and

Charles Sage, when his launch capsized off South Mala. At Norfolk Island a boy was washed off the rocks and carried two miles out to sea and Walter Long swam out to him and helped to bring him ashore, only to lose his own life landing on the rocks in the surf. More recently, David Hoey and David Clunies Ross were drowned when their launch capsized in a heavy sea. But we all had our boats capsized sometimes in surf landings. We all learnt both to fear and love the sea. I love it best from the land.

One of our Bishops was once landing in a dinghy at a dangerous place on San Cristoval, where the surf banks up in a narrow channel. He had with him his Archdeacon and two women, both Europeans, a nurse and a teacher, and two lads to paddle the dinghy. The dinghy was overwhelmed by a big surf and all were in the water. Neither the Archdeacon nor the nurse could swim. The former clung to the dinghy and was rescued exhausted. The nurse was rescued very bravely by the Bishop and brought to land. It was a place where sharks were very numerous because cattle were slaughtered nearby on the plantation and the party were fortunate that all came through safely.

To return to Burgess. He was the greatest of all our captains and knew the island waters as no one else has, and the many reefs, charted and uncharted, where so many island ships have come to grief. He would often row about taking soundings when we were at anchor, and no one else was so careful to give us a good lee when we came aboard in a rough sea. Once at Ulawa the Bishop was very late coming aboard and we went across to Mala twenty miles away on a very dark and stormy night. We could not even see the white of the surf as we neared the narrow entrance to Port Adam, but after we had put out all lights he took the ship straight in and anchored at our usual anchorage. It must have been by smell. Only once did I know him to make a mistake. I was to have been landed at Heuru on the west end of San Cristoval. It was another black night of wind and sea and driving rain, and Burgess sent me ashore in the ship's boat six miles to the east of the right place. I jumped from the boat on to the black sand beach, and they rowed back to the ship which went on. I did not know the beach and struggled up it and over the crest into a river in flood running parallel to the beach. I scrambled somehow out of that and walked along in the rain to a heathen village where they would not let me stay in one of the houses because I was a Christian, but allowed me to sleep in a small and leaky leaf shed wherein were creeping things innumerable. Next morning after a poor night I walked along to Heuru.

That was a rare mistake for Burgess to make. He was a man very loyal to the Mission and he and Bishop Steward were great friends. His Melanesian crew would do anything for him and followed him year after year. When the time came at last for *Southern Cross V* to be given up and *Southern Cross VI* was rebuilt in England to replace her, we took it for granted that Burgess would be her captain, and Bishop Steward had given him a written promise that he would command her. In later years I read the letters that passed between the Mission Committee in England and the Committee in New Zealand. The English Committee had wished for Burgess but the New Zealand Committee insisted, for personal reasons I believe, on a new captain. So the Mission lost a great and loyal captain. We did not see his like again.

On *Southern Cross V* was a very beautiful chapel with a mosaic of Christ walking on the water, at the back of the altar. This chapel was divided from the saloon by sliding doors so that when these slid back we had a small church. One day while we were at Mattins and singing lustily "Onward Christian Soldiers", a cow, bent on exploration, came up the alleyway aft of the saloon and joined in the hymn. The alleyway was too narrow for her to retire so some of us brought her into the congregation, turned her round and sent her home again. The congregation sang on, rather distracted, for the cow had no idea of the tune.

We were once anchored at Tulagi when the *Southern Cross V* was asked to tow across the harbour a two-thousand-ton Finnish barque, four times our size. Exactly what happened I do not know but somehow we got entangled with the barque at right angles, with her bowsprit right across us forward while both ships were at rest. This large bowsprit moved slowly aft removing whatever it found in its path, with the sailors on the barque all talking excitedly in

Finnish and our lads in Mota. Our mate called to me in an agitated voice to push off the barque but I found two thousand tons too much for me. The bowsprit moved majestically along removing things. It swept off the rails on our bridge while our Melanesian steersman knelt underneath apparently in prayer. It moved up against our funnel and there it came to rest satisfied with what it had done. Everyone was shouting in Finnish, Mota and English except the captain. A small steamer came to our rescue and our bowsprit, following the example of its big sister, did the same thing to our rescuer. We were all tangled up together and none of us could move lest a worse thing should befall us. In the end the tide drifted us apart and we went off to lick our wounds.

As a member of the native Brotherhood I travelled a great deal on *Southern Cross VII* after *Southern Cross VI* was wrecked. She was only half the size of *Southern Cross V* but an excellent little ship. Once we came to Anuda, about seventy miles from Tikopia, and a very isolated island, never visited except by our ship, and by her only once a year. The landing there in the surf is one of the worst in Melanesia and often impossible. On that occasion it was quite impossible, but the Bishop did not like to go on as the people have no priest and can only get the sacraments when we call there. So we lay off in a heavy sea for several days hoping that conditions would improve, but at last the Bishop decided it was hopeless and we must go on. And then we saw the congregation coming out to us, men and women, forcing their way through the heavy surf and swimming out, each with a log to help him through the rough sea. It was a long swim and a hard one, but one by one they reached us and climbed on board, changed into white loin-cloths, made their communion, and dived in again and swam home. I cannot imagine European communicants either capable of this or doing it if they could.

On another occasion we were in the Banks Group, and going from Maewo to Vanualava met with very heavy weather, a fierce south-easter. The boys slept aft on the deck, the distance was about fifty miles, and all that night the deck was awash. They had a wretched night and none turned up in the morning for the daily Eucharist. "Well," said the Bishop, "they must have Mattins," and he went up on the deck to take it, giving out as the office hymn:

> My Father, for another night
> Of quiet sleep and rest. . . .

Melanesians have a keen sense of humour, and they sang heartily.

Several times we visited Rennell and Bellona, two isolated islands fifty miles to the south of the Solomons. These are very interesting islands, off the beaten track, with a Polynesian-speaking people, their language akin more to Maori than to Samoan or Tongan, though they are Micronesian in physical character. Rennell is a coral island raised four hundred feet, fifty-six miles long, with a lovely lake twelve miles long at its southern end, round which most of the people live. I once paddled the whole length of it. It has no fish but many eels and the water is brackish but the people dig wells beside it. On the rest of the island there is very little fresh water, for the rain sinks away in the coral. There are large gardens of pawpaws, the people's chief food. In Bishop Patteson's day some boys from these islands went to the Mission school in Auckland about 1860 but in later years it was hardly visited. Bishop Wilson went there twice. When I went there in Bishop Baddeley's time the islands were new ground to us. Whalers used to call there and the first thing the chief asked me was how many women the Bishop wanted for the night. We had anchored at the only Rennell anchorage, White Sands, and climbed the steep cliffs to the plateau and lake, for no one lives on the shore.

We did not stay long that time, but went on to Bellona, a few miles away, and lay off the shore. The Bishop and I and our companion Bill Seaton went ashore in the boat, and found a crowd of men on the shore, but no women. Numbers of men were running along towards us and there was a noisy and not very friendly crowd round us. With our party was a young Tikopian who could understand their talk, but suddenly he ran to the reef, dived in and swam out to the ship. He told us afterwards that he had heard someone say: "Give them a basket of fish, and when they sit down to eat it, kill them." He did not tell us but said he thought it best to go. The crowd was getting noisy, some tried to snatch off the Bishop's pectoral cross, while others threw their arms round Bill, who was fat and well liking; and no women appeared, which is always a warning to be careful. I told the Bishop we had better go quietly to the boat and row off, which we did. I don't think they meant anything serious, and now they are used to white men. Perhaps something had happened to upset them.

My own first stay at Rennell was accidental and involuntary. Our ship had anchored at White Sands, and two of us of the Native Brotherhood went ashore in the boat to try and make contact with the people when they came down the cliffs. We then knew nothing about them, not even if they were friendly or hostile. The boat went back to the ship and left us ashore. A sudden and severe storm blew up and the captain blew three or four toots on his whistle and the ship went off to the other side of the island for shelter, leaving us there for three or four days to meet and get to know the people, some of whom presently began to climb down the cliffs to see who we were. They proved to be friendly and we slept with them and tried to get to know their language. We lived on cooked pawpaws and climbed the cliffs and saw their village and met the two chiefs, Takua and Tapongi, before the ship came back; and we made friends with some of them, especially a lad named Buia, who became one of my best friends. Later some of their lads came to our school at Tabalia and when these returned others came for some time to a school we had at Alangkaula. When these were taken home they were very anxious to return to us, but the ship had ceased to visit Rennell, so six of them got hold of an old dugout canoe and set off across fifty miles of open sea to get back to us. And they did, first to San Cristoval and then round the coast of that island and across to Ugi, where our school was. It was a most adventurous voyage.

The Bishop asked the Government to let me go and live on Rennell, without any calls from the ship lest we should introduce sickness, in order that I might study the language and customs of the people. But the Government said this would not be fair to other Missions who wanted to go there and in the end we ceased to visit these islands and left them to others.

The Native names of the two islands are Munggava and Munggiki i.e. Big Mu and Little Mu. I am told that at Tuamotu, on the eastern fringe of Polynesia, thousands of miles from Rennell and Bellona, there is a tradition that their ancestors came from the land of Mu. Is this some place in Indonesia? The Rennell and Bellona people speak a language very like Maori except that the Maori letter r is *ngg* (like *ng* in *linger*), and I think the first of them probably came down from Micronesia, when the Polynesians were passing through those islands to their present home. Others may have come later from Uvea in Polynesia. This would account for the fact that physically their characteristics are said to be Micronesian though they speak a Polynesian tongue. They have no canoes except the poorest dugouts.

Some men from Tikopia once reached them about thirty or forty years ago. The Tikopians are very adventurous people. When out fishing in their canoes some of the canoes are blown away nearly every year, and are either never heard of again or manage to make some other island far away. In this way some have reached Santa Cruz and the Reef Islands, some have reached and settled in the Banks Islands and some have even got to Santo in the New Hebrides, several hundred miles. One such canoe of castaways managed to reach Rennell, five hundred miles distant. They told me they landed there at night, wondering what strange island they had come to, and climbed the cliffs in the dark. They were very nervous, fearing they had come to hostile people, and took refuge in a tree near the village till daylight should come and they could see the people. As it got light the people began to come out of their houses, but then a branch broke on which the Tikopians were standing and they were discovered. To their joy they found a friendly people speaking a language they could understand, and they lived with them for two or three years till Bishop Wilson arrived in *Southern Cross V* and took them home to Tikopia, where they had long been given up as dead.

CHAPTER TEN

SMALL SHIPS

MUCH of our travelling in the Solomons has been done in small ships and whaleboats, often in rough seas. The first ketch owned by the Mission was the *Selwyn* which was sailed down from New Zealand. I seldom travelled in her. She was used by the Archdeacon in his visitations, just as an archdeacon in civilisation uses a motor car. But when *Southern Cross VI* was wrecked and there was no Mission ship for a year, the Bishop himself had to use a small ship, and get about as best he could. His favourite little ship was the *William Voy*, a small ketch with an engine, which wallowed along steadily at four or five knots. I was on her with the Bishop a good deal. The Bishop himself was new, with no knowledge of a ship, although he was a splendid sailor and quite unaffected by rough weather.

What interested me about *William Voy* was the number of captains we had, I mean at one and the same time. The nominal captain was a New Zealand farmer who had just joined the Mission. However because of his inexperience on the sea there was a Melanesian with him who was at home on a ketch. The Melanesian did not much like giving orders; when our farmer gave an order (usually in a low and uncertain voice) our Melanesian captain did not really take much notice of it. He rather retired into himself. There was a third whom I should call captain of our sails. He pulled them up or down as seemed to him best. So it was too with the captain of our engine, who went ahead or astern when the fancy took him. The captain of our anchor dropped it from time to time when it seemed to him a good idea. And thus we wallowed about from island to island, with never more than forty miles of open sea, but often difficult navigation among the reefs and shoals. The Bishop supposed it was all normal, being new to the Mission. He was a man to enjoy every new experience to the full.

Once when we were at Ulawa Island the Bishop was so much delayed by his work ashore that we did not leave till dark for the next place on our list, which was Pawa School on Ugi about thirty miles away. The Bishop had not yet met the headmaster. It was a black night, with heavy rain and violent squalls, but we managed to make Ugi soon after midnight, though in the rain it was barely visible. Somehow we stumbled into Selwyn Bay. We did not know whereabouts in the bay we were and it is three miles across. There was shelter here from the wind, but not from the driving rain, and it was a black night. After the captain of the anchor had decided to drop it—as it happened just in time, close to some rocks—I said I would go ashore in the dinghy and find out where we were. I came back and told the Bishop we were at the wrong end of the bay, more than two miles from the school, and suggested we should wait for morning. But not the Bishop! "Let us go ashore and walk along," he said. It was about 2 a.m. So he and I and Ini Kopuria pulled ashore in the dinghy and set out for the school, I holding an umbrella in one hand and a hurricane lantern in the other, followed by the Bishop and Ini, for I knew the way. Presently we came to a stream, usually quite small, but I had forgotten the days of rain. "All right, Bishop," I said, "its quite shallow," and stepped in over my head, the lantern going out as I sat on the umbrella and disappeared under the water. I struggled out across the stream, not much wetter than before, and the Bishop followed me as soon as he could stop laughing, and we went up the hill to Pawa School. As I expected, the headmaster was sleeping on the verandah. It was pitch dark, three dripping figures approached the bed, and I put my hand on the headmaster's head and said to him, "Richard, let me introduce you to our new Bishop".

We had lots of fun on *William Voy* and our guardian angels had a busy time.

A later Bishop also had to begin his work without a ship in which to visit his diocese. While he was waiting for a new *Southern Cross* to be built he had to use a launch called *Mavis*, or a ketch *Selwyn* 2. One December, which is our monsoon season, he had been all round Ysabel in *Selwyn* 2 with the Archdeacon. The island is a hundred and twenty miles long and the monsoon had started early; the weather was atrocious, most of the time they were fighting gales and wet through. They really had a bad time. But they decided to continue their travels, monsoon or not, and go all round Mala, where conditions might be worse, and the Bishop was kind enough to ask me to join them. He also invited our missionary in charge of Mala. Selwyn is small, and the cabin was full of stores and luggage, so we all had to live and sleep aft on the deck in a very small space, just enough room, and no more, to set up two deck chairs. The Archdeacon said at once that from boyhood he had always loathed a deck chair, and liked something hard such as the deck or the top of the cabin. The Bishop and the man from Mala both seemed to feel the same. This did not really surprise me, knowing all three of them as I did; it left me, if I wished, the choice of two deck chairs; but in the end we made the Bishop have one of them. Nor did it surprise me that if there was an extra bit of work, or some unpleasant job to be done, the Bishop would rush to do it—that is if he could get to it before the Archdeacon, which was unlikely. So for me everything was made easy, pleasant and quiet.

All except Selwyn herself, for she is a ship that very much dislikes even a small ripple on her beam. It irritates her, upsets her in every sense; she flies into a rage and throws herself about. What she likes is a perfectly calm sea and a gentle following breeze and then, and then only, she goes along quietly at five knots. We had this only once in the four weeks we lived on her. The Bishop had once been a sailor, captain of an ocean liner, so he knew all about nautical matters and told me at once before we boarded her that Selwyn was very likely to open out and sink if we got into a rough sea, which of course we were sure to do. But he was wrong about that. She did take in a lot of water in rough weather, but it was through the pump, down which we poured bucket after bucket of sea water to make it work, which it never did. Still Selwyn seemed to enjoy the fifty buckets or so of water which we poured into her, and went on happily, refreshed by her drink.

Our first anchorage was at our hospital on Mala, forty miles from where I was picked up; but it is no anchorage in a monsoon, and *Selwyn* fled to a better place ten miles north of us, with all her canvas torn off her; returning later looking quite bare. The Melanesian crew spent a day sewing fresh canvas. We walked along some ten miles and *Selwyn* picked us up and rolled us along to Fiu and a very bad surf landing; and so we went on round the island.

Sometimes we went ashore and climbed the hills to a bush village. At the age of seventy-seven I found these hills steeper than they used to be. The Bishop and Archdeacon would leap like young goats up an eight hundred foot hill, very steep and rough, while I followed more like a turtle on land. Bishop Steward always used to say Melanesia needed two Bishops, one for "Lower Melanesia" and one for "Upper Melanesia".

At one place on the coast the Bishop confirmed some people; but four who had been prepared were not presented by the Catechist as he thought they were not yet ready; so their friends beat him up for not presenting them. Vicars at home should not let this story get about. At another place the Bishop laid his hands on a man possessed by a devil. Forty years ago, when the people were heathen, possession by evil spirits used to be common, but it has gradually ceased as they became Christians, and is rarely seen now. In ordinary cases of mental disease we lay hands on our people. Bishop Steward did not give us a form of Unction because he thought Melanesian priests would not keep the oil carefully, but he wrote, and had printed in our Prayer Book, a form for laying on of hands. He himself used this often both for mental and bodily illness. Once a woman who was insane was brought to me at Fiu. The doctor had said nothing could be done for her. I had her carried to my house and asked two or three good Christians to come in with me. She was raving and throwing herself about, but when I laid my hands on her she became quiet and sane; and has remained so.

Among the heathen in earlier days we did see many cases of possession such as one reads about in the Bible. Possessed people are immensely strong; they throw themselves into the fire and into the water; they dash through the forest at night without

hitting anything. I was once with one of these whom about twelve
men were trying to hold down, and I had with me a doctor, a
visitor. I asked him what he thought about it. He said it was a
"nervous disease not found in civilisation". A Melanesian friend
writes, "The evil spirit enters into a man like this: he gazes about
him for a while as if he were afraid, then he rises up and stiffens
his whole body, and beats with his fists on trees or on his body,
and no one else is able to come near him. Once some men, perhaps
about ten, tried to grapple with a possessed man, but he broke
clear of them. When he does these things he cries and weeps;
spittle comes out of his mouth, his body is bloodied; if there
is a fire near and it reaches him he does not feel it at all. He goes
on like this until he prophesies like the prophets we have learned
about. I have seen three men possessed like this by evil spirits."
That is a fair description of what we used to see. The modern
Melanesian Christians have forgotten what it was like. The devils
have been cast out. We now take this to be metaphor only.

So gradually Selwyn worked her way round Mala. The monsoon
was always threatening. Once as soon as we got into the open
sea we found huge swells growing bigger all the time and a bank
of black clouds coming up from the north west, so we had to
turn back into a harbour and wait for the storm to pass. We
visited other islands; Ulawa, San Cristoval, and Ugi, about thirty
miles apart, always hoping the weather would hold till we got
across. It generally did. After a month of this we were home
again. People in New Zealand always tell us how good it must
be to spend so much of our time yachting, and I think some
of them would enjoy it.

I have been round Mala too with a recruiter. Recruiters are
men seeking native labour for the coconut plantations; they
also travel in small ships in much the same way as we do, but
in that ship we refreshed ourselves with beer, I think about once
every hour. They are generally excellent men and see Melanesians
from a different point of view. They bring trade and get a warm
welcome from the people. I enjoyed that voyage, in much better
weather than we had in the Selwyn, and my companions in that

ship also were very pleasant people to travel with. Sometimes of course we ran on a reef. There are lots of them about and so generally we don't travel by night.

The present Archdeacon enjoys, or says he does, going about the Group in a small launch in very bad weather. He is a very good sailor and adds to his excitements by not being able to swim. After a voyage in our little launch *Mavis* and a wild time on a black night with a howling gale and torrential rain he remarked (in the Mission magazine) that these voyages remind him of the words of the hymn:

> "The trivial round, the common task
> Should furnish all we need to ask".

I never used to ask for these things myself.

Most of my travels have been by whaleboat. I had three islands to look after. I used to go right round San Cristoval, about two hundred miles, every three months; and occasionally go over to Mala and Ulawa, thirty miles away. I had a lug sail but you can't beat up against the wind with this and we generally had to row. I had a crew of eight, four to row and four to take a spell, while I managed the eighteen-foot steer oar. If the blade gets flat and the water begins to press it down it is apt to stand up vertically before you know where you are. A fellow missionary, unused to the devil in steer oars, got caught, in his pants, and the oar went steadily vertical, suspending him at a height of several feet above his boat. Very embarrassing.

You get many landings in heavy surf and it takes experience to judge the right wave to come in on. If you misjudge, your boat gets swamped and probably turns over. You must have patience to wait. It is especially difficult at night, when you can't see the breakers coming up behind you, and a big one may take you by surprise; and you need, too, more weight than I have behind the steer oar. But I only turned my boat over once, and that was when I was trying to show off. A visitor from England was with us. I had been a long journey in the boat down the coast and was coming home, and the English visitor was waiting on the beach. I thought I would show him how we in Melanesia come in through a heavy surf. I did!—the boat upside down and all of us swimming. If there are no rocks about it does not matter very much.

Once when I was coming home in the boat from Santa Ana, an island fifty miles down the coast, we had to face a north-west monsoon which got worse and worse all day as we rowed on steadily against it, doing about two knots—quite good going. Night came on and we were still nowhere near a place where we could land. About nine o'clock my crew said we must put ashore somewhere for they were too tired to go on after rowing all day against the monsoon. There *was* a possible landing near there, at a place called Rumatari, but it was very difficult, a winding passage through the reef, on which there would be a big sea with the gale that was blowing; and the night was so black you could hardly see your hand before your face, and a driving rain was making things worse. However I said we would try. We blew on our shell so that the people ashore might show a light, but they thought we were a war canoe, common in those days, and retired to the hills. I turned the boat towards where I hoped the landing was and in we went, high and dry up on the beach on top of a big breaker. In the morning I found we had come in at the wrong place, on the crest of that wave, over boulders the size of a kitchen table. However all was well; and it is not all like that. I remember fresh clear mornings rowing along the weather coast in calm weather past lovely little sandy coves; or after a long night of rain and cold in the boat seeing the sun rise over the sea. Pleasant memories. I had about ten years of travel in my whaleboat. In this a sea diocese we get to know the sea in all its moods.

Canoes are still in general use, but there are no longer many large ones, and you no longer, or only rarely, see fleets of them. The people are buying launches. But a former missionary told me he had seen a hundred large war canoes, with about twenty armed men in each, setting out on an expedition. I have seen no more than thirty. Most are made of planks sewn together, the seams covered with black gum, with high prow and stern. I have seen one such, beautifully inlaid, which held sixty men. Such a canoe can travel at six or seven knots, and is a fine sight as the brown bodies sway in unison, changing their stroke from time to time as the man at the bow does so. Ysabel men are the finest canoe men, and they are not afraid to face a storm at sea. There is no pleasanter way of travelling except that one is rather cramped.

There are still plenty of small ones, some built of planks and some dugouts, some one-man, some two or three or five-man canoes. They cannot, or could not, be bought with English money. There were three things for which native red shell money (strings of red disks) was necessary: a canoe, a pig, and a wife.

I often travelled by canoe and only once had an accident. When I was at Pamua I set off one Saturday in a small one-man canoe to the point at the other end of the big bay, about five miles away. It was an old canoe, with the front plank missing, so I sat well back to bring the bow up. However this brought the stern low and when I was about a mile and a half from land a squall came up and my canoe filled and sank. A Melanesian might have managed to bale it out and climb in, but this was beyond me, so I took off my clothes and set out for the shore; it is a lonely feeling out at sea by oneself, and it took some time to swim ashore. When I got within two hundred yards a Melanesian fishing further along the beach noticed me and ran along and swam out to help me through the surf, though I did not need any help. I landed near a river mouth and he asked me, "Didn't you think of the sharks and crocodiles? There are lots about here." But I had clean forgotten them, and had only thought it seemed a long way; and was annoyed chiefly at losing a tattered old felt hat I had long been wearing.

CHAPTER ELEVEN

TRAVELS ON LAND

I WAS much more at home on the land than on the sea. I had walked over most of the North Island in New Zealand, but Melanesia is rather different, with no roads, only narrow tracks full of roots and rocks. Because of the roots in the paths Melanesians lift their feet high in walking; Europeans, accustomed to smooth roads do not, and so in Melanesia continually stumble. It is amusing to see Melanesians who go to New Zealand lifting their feet high on a smooth road. They also walk in single file because the tracks are narrow, and are so used to this that they do so even on a broad road.

The hills are very steep, covered with thick forest; sometimes there are thick clumps of bamboos for several miles, sometimes you have to walk for miles through mangrove country up to your knees in black mud. The rivers can be difficult as there is heavy rainfall and they flood quickly; you may be caught in a rocky gorge by a sudden rise of water. There is often now a road along the coast, but once coast walking was difficult, in places impossible, in others tramping through soft black sand.

I generally walked alone, sometimes with a Melanesian friend. Once on the high mountains of San Cristoval I lost my way completely, and had to find the beginning of a river and follow it down to the sea, no easy matter. Even Melanesians have been lost in the hills, and have died before they could be found. Up on those high hills I used to admire the profusion of ground orchids, red, white, and purple. Once a Melanesian friend brought me a magnificent orchid; there were masses of blooms on the plant, each two or three inches across, rich ruddy brown in colour with deep black velvety markings. I tried to grow it, but it came from the high hills and failed to live on the coast, and I never saw another.

97

G

One of my most usual walks was across San Cristoval at its narrowest, from Wango to Bia. It is only about twelve miles. You follow a shallow river, crossing and recrossing it as the track lies on one side or the other, sometimes following the river bed for some distance, a rocky bed with water only two or three feet deep. Finally you climb a saddle and descend by a very steep and rough path over volcanic rocks and scoria to the sea on the other side of the island. It always took me four hours, with breakfast at Wango and lunch at Bia. But others less used to it were apt to take longer.

Once one of our Bishops came to me when I was living at Wango. He had been visiting his diocese in a whaleboat, had done five hundred miles in the boat in all sorts of weather during several weeks, and he and his crew were tired. He wanted to visit the villages on the other side of San Cristoval, but it was seventy miles round by sea, so I suggested he should walk across to Bia and then visit the villages on the other side by canoe. I was laid up with a tropical ulcer and could not go with him. "But," I said, "you just follow the river most of the way, crossing it sometimes, and then go over the saddle and there you are." He told me afterwards he counted the times he crossed the river—sixty-two times according to him.

He had with him his chaplain, just out from England. Both were wearing new brown shoes, not good for river walking; the chaplain was new to Melanesia, and the Bishop, most lovable of bishops, was stout and jolly. With his glasses he looked rather like Mr. Pickwick. I think they took ten hours. The sharp pebbles in the river bed got into their shoes and made their feet so sore that they decided to walk barefoot. But that was worse, and by the time they came to the steep scoria descent they were limping very painfully. The Bishop felt he could not walk down that very steep and rough scoria slope; so he sat down on the edge and slid down very fast. This removed the part of his pants he was sitting on, and it was very embarrassing because at the bottom was the village, two rows of houses at right angles to the sea, and the people standing at the doors to welcome him, and he was not in a fit state to be seen. Holding on to what was left he trotted steadily between the people, straight into the sea, and sat down in the water. The village teacher approached him nervously.

"Father, the people are all waiting to shake hands."

The Bishop replied, "Tell the people to go inside and shut their doors, and the Bishop will come out of the sea."

Some people tell me I ought not to tell this story because it shows disrespect to my Bishop. I would never wish to do that. I respected that Bishop deeply. I loved him too, because he was so human, and one of the most understanding men I have had the good luck to know; but he often told the story himself—although he never, perhaps, forgave me for advising him to take the path across the island. He came back the seventy miles by canoe.

I once spent a good deal of time at Bia. I had walked across, barefoot as I always went, and the walk did no good to an ulcer on my leg, so that I had to wait at Bia for a month before it healed enough for me to go on. I lay on a mat in a leaf house with a bit of red calico (all they had) wrapped round the leg to keep the flies off. During the day people would come in and chat and go away again. The house was full of village dogs, mangy and thin, and sometimes pigs came in, to be chased out again by the dogs. It was January, when food is very scarce, for the yam crop is not dug till Easter, and in January and February there is not very much to eat. I lived on green bananas broiled on the embers. They are bitter, but I used to shut my eyes and say, "This is a sausage," or, "a juicy steak". They are not bad that way. Indeed I have never spent a more pleasant month, getting to know the village people well, and greatly improving my knowledge of the language.

I had a very enjoyable walk once with another Bishop in New Britain. We left the Mission ship and went by launch fifteen miles up a river and then sent the launch back and walked seventy miles parallel to the shore through the interior of the island; and then walked down to the coast and were picked up again. This was quite different from my walks on San Cristoval because a Bishop takes about twenty boys to carry beds, pots and pans and food. It was quite luxurious. The Bishop tramped steadily along, and I about two yards behind, as becomes a priest with his Bishop. He had once been a colonel in the army, so we walked army style, fifty minutes walking and then ten minutes spell. When it came to the spell woe betide the boy who was not at hand with a deckchair when the Bishop wanted to sit down. We came to one very nasty place, a canyon about twelve feet across, with sheer rock walls down to a river far below rushing over jagged rocks. There was a small tree growing on the edge and the boys cut it down so that it fell across the canyon. But it was a very small tree, with just room for one's foot and no more. The Bishop went first, with a boy in front and another behind to hold him steady. I believe he shut his eyes. I came behind crawling shamelessly on hands and knees. But the weight of the Bishop and two boys was rather too much and as we got to the middle our bridge gave a loud crack. However it did not break, and the Melanesians skipped over behind us like mountain goats. We came to another river, very broad and deep. This time the boys made a raft, quite small, to ferry us over one by one. The Bishop, however, had an extra boy to steady him so the raft was weighed down, and he crossed on it sitting in a foot of water. It took some time to ferry us all across one by one. This was a charming walk— new country, picturesque natives, war dances, all that one could wish for on a walk, and a good track and easy walking.

When walking along the coast the rivers can be a nuisance because they are full of crocodiles. If I came to a river which it was necessary to swim, and saw a crocodile in the river, I used to throw stones at it till it disappeared, take off my clothes, put them on a log, and swim across pushing the log. You may feel anxious about your toes and inclined to draw them in, but it is not as dangerous as it sounds, because crocodiles are nervous animals and don't attack unless they are sure there will be no trouble; they prefer pigs and dogs. I was once crossing a San Cristoval river with a Melanesian who was holding his dog in his arms when a crocodile rose and took the dog but did not harm us. The people say they are afraid of anything white, but I never felt sure about this. They have a special way of getting rid of a crocodile that has made its home in a stream near their village. First they peel the bark off thin strips cut from the branches of a tree, so that these strips become white wands. Then, taking these with them, the young men swim off up the river until they meet the crocodile, who sees the white wands and flees from them. And so they drive it on to the shore, where the whole village attacks it and kills it with axes.

I have heard, on reliable authority from a man whom I never knew to exaggerate, of a crocodile over thirty feet in length, but the largest I ever saw was twenty-four feet, and generally they are only eight to twelve feet long. The best way to see them is when they are on the mud and don't hear any suspicious sound. They stand up on their feet, with backs hunched up, looking like prehistoric monsters, and walk slowly along, but at the first sound they go flat on their bellies and slither away. Once two of us were in a dinghy floating quietly down a river close to a six foot grassy bank, when suddenly a crocodile leaped from the top of the bank, clean over us, with a great splash. Sometimes they go some distance inland through the forest, and I have known one try to climb a tree after a boy, the trunk being sloping; and the boy going very fast to the top of the tree.

At Bungana Girls' School there was a crocodile who appeared to be friendly and used to come up into the school grounds, but the girls never quite trusted it. The headmistress was said to have made a rule that it must not come into the girls' dormitories. In former days certain crocodiles were worshipped, and the people in those villages could certainly walk into the water among them without any fear. It is said there was one at Siota on Gela which used to ferry its friends across the mile of water between Siota and Boromole. A Belaga man, that is, one of its own people, would come to Siota and call it and sit on its back for the ride across!

It was at Boromole that a lad was taken by a crocodile a year or two ago. He came down to the sea in the very early morning, sat down on a fallen coconut log, and began to light his pipe. A crocodile in the bushes behind leaped on him and bit a piece out of his thigh and shoved him into four feet of water. They rose together, Paul hugging the crocodile round its belly and holding on tight, while the crocodile reared up several feet above Paul's head and clawed his shoulders with its forefeet. The people came running up in answer to Paul's shouts and drove the crocodile off. Paul got to hospital in about forty-eight hours, by canoe and launch, and recovered. But wrestling with one of these slimy beasts would not be to my fancy!

Another lad was taken in the Wairaha River in San Cristoval, a river I often used to swim across. He was going home from school for his holiday and had to swim the river, where a crocodile seized him by the thigh, carried him under water, and tucked him away in a mud bank, meaning to come back for him at leisure when he had become more tasty. But Matthias was not dead and managed to come to the surface and swim to where the bank was low. He told me that this was his worst moment, when he found he had not strength to crawl out, and expected the crocodile to come back for him. However some people found him and brought him in a canoe to our hospital on Ugi, where I saw the deep holes made by the crocodile's teeth in his thigh. They became septic, but healed in time, and Matthias can delight again in his favourite game as wing forward at soccer.

Crocodiles are to be avoided, but they do not give me the same feeling of repulsion as the very big spiders, which drop on you with their soft weight at night when you are sleeping in a native house. Probably everyone has his own special dislike. When I was a member of the Native Brotherhood there came to us from Kelham Father J., a deeply loved priest of the Mission. We had prepared a leaf house for him, and at bedtime I took him to it. Before long I heard wild shouting from the house and hurried over. What I saw was Father J. standing in his pyjamas on the native bed, shouting and violently opening and shutting an umbrella at a large land crab which was gazing solemnly at him from the floor. He never really got over his dislike of these land crabs, which come down to the sea once a year in a great moving mass of many thousands, to spawn and then return to the hills. A year or two later when Father J. was celebrating the Eucharist at a boys' school he saw one of these crabs walking slowly up the aisle towards him. What the startled congregation heard was: "Hear also what St. John saith; will no one take that crab out of the church?"

On San Cristoval I often used to go off for a month among the hill people, then all heathen. I used in those days to go barefoot and bareheaded, wearing a loin-cloth and singlet, and taking nothing except a small native bag slung on my shoulder, in which were my pipe and one book for solid reading. The hill people were very friendly and entertained me freely. The rule of hospitality among them is to entertain for three days anyone who comes; after that they give him no food. Anyone I met would give me a little bit of native tobacco for my pipe. In the evenings we sat round fires in their houses and talked.

One incident stands out in San Cristoval walks. It was when the terrible sickness after the First World War reached the island, and scores of people were dying in the villages. The people were so frightened that they had left their villages and built leaf shelters in the hills behind, and I was visiting these clusters of shelters one after another, to talk to the sick and dying. As I came out of one there met me four men carrying a bier on which lay a dying man. They put it down so that I could talk to him. As I was leaving him he said, looking up at me, "I am very cold, give me your singlet". I gave it to him and as they put it on him he looked up at me with an expression in his eyes of great kindness towards me which I cannot describe and cannot ever forget; a long, keen, quiet look. He died and was buried five minutes later. A week or two later someone in a village gave me another singlet.

The hill people were normally healthy, because each village was built on the round top of a hill, free from mosquitoes. You could shout across the valley between that and another village on the next hill. Across the top of the hill was a deep ditch, perhaps thirty feet deep and a hundred yards long and too broad to jump across. A long log lay across it for them to pass over, so that if the enemy attacked one part of the village the people ran across to the other part and pulled the log after them. In one village I met a famous fighting chief who had held the end of the bridge against the enemy for a long time till all the people had passed over safely, and then had sprung across the ditch with a mighty leap; a Melanesian Horatius. It was pleasant to meet him and hear him describe it all.

The Government officers brought these people down from their hills to the shore so that they could tax them more easily. But life on the shore was fatal to them; a different sort of food and climate and many mosquitoes. Last of all the Marching Rule movement called them down. There are few hill villages left now; and the population of San Cristoval cannot be half of what it was a hundred years ago. But it is once more on the increase.

CHAPTER TWELVE

GELA

THE name is properly Nggela, but we usually write and pronounce it with the initial G. I began to learn the Gela language from Gela boys at our Norfolk Island school. In later years, when living in Gela villages, I wrote a dictionary of about 15,000 words and a grammar,* and collected Gela folk stories. The language is worth comparing with the language of Nias in Western Sumatra, both in grammar and vocabulary.

The people have totem clans like the people of Arosi, but they are not bird clans and there is no special clan of the chiefs. In a village the senior member of the clan which is most numerous is the village chief. So if the chief happens to belong to the Kakau (Crab) clan (descent being reckoned from the mother who is not Kakau), in the next generation some other clan will be more numerous, and the Chief will belong to that.

The Gela people are different from those of other islands, and I have always had a special affection for them. The women have great influence. A man's wife decides where the next crop is to be planted, and how large the garden is to be. She is "Lord of the garden". She is also called "Lord of the reef", and she knows far more about it than the men do. Being a conchologist, I used to go to the women to get the Gela names of the shells. On one beach about a hundred yards long I found forty-six species of Conus.

Every Gela man has his farm from which he gets a living for himself and his family. The clan owns the land, but every member of it has enough for his own use for as long as he lives, and probably his son will inherit it and farm it. The people also own the reefs. Native shell money was made at Auke Island on Mala, twenty-five miles across the sea from Gela, but the Mala people have always come

* Published by the Auckland Museum.

across to get the shell from which they make the white disks of the shell money, because this shell (an arca) is abundant on the Gela reefs, and they have always paid a fee to the Gela people who live opposite the particular reef on which they are fishing for the shells. This is an important point, because Europeans have considered the reefs to be public property, and have fished for Trochus shell without paying the owners of the reef any fee. But the reefs are open to all except for shellfish that have a money value; just as anyone can cut down trees on native land if they are not "valuable", e.g. for food or canoes or houses, which alone are property.

The people of Gela will tell you that they were never cannibals, but when the Spaniards went there four hundred years ago, Mendana described them as ferocious cannibals. The Spaniards landed and took what food they needed, and Mendana complains that the inhabitants objected and retreated to the hills, and that some of them threw spears at the visitors and had to be shot because of their warlike attitude. It is interesting that some of their other customs seem to have changed, for Mendana says they dyed their hair red, but Brook, the first white man to live among them a hundred years ago, says their custom was to shave their heads, leaving one tuft, while the Mala people left their hair untouched. Stranger still, Mendana says they built their villages over the water. In Brook's time, three hundred years later, there was not a case of this, nor even the memory of it. But the Mala custom of building villages over water, said to have begun some three hundred years ago, may perhaps have originated on Gela. But why did the Gela people give it up?

Gela is a beautiful island, the most beautiful in the Solomons, with many fine harbours. Through the island runs a narrow and deep strait, no wider than a river, and winding about, with forest-covered hills on each side, a safe and short way through for ships up to five hundred tons. The old name is Scudamore Passage, but it is now called the Boli Pass. The Gela name is Utucha. The last four miles at the western end open out into a fine harbour, Purvis Harbour, where during the war, I once counted more than two hundred American warships and transports, with many small launches dashing about between them, like a busy harbour in civilisation. Now it is quiet and deserted. There is only a small wharf at the Mission Headquarters, and a solitary little launch tied up to it. It was here after the 1914 war that Admiral Jellicoe, who visited the islands then, proposed to have a great British naval base, but the British Government hoped then that no war would come. Scores of Americans used to swim across the Boli Pass when they had a naval base at Siota in the last war. On the hills that border the passage are wonderful limestone caves, discovered by Captain Hilder but still unexplored. They are said to rival the finest caves elsewhere.

Gela is not all forested like most of the islands; grass-covered hills are found everywhere, which are supposed to be due to salt deposits in the soil. Along the shores of the deep bays are mangrove forests in the water, with deep winding channels through them to the solid land. Going to Gumu, an inland village, you follow one of these narrow ways through mangroves for a mile or so, and then several miles more of a passage through beautiful niva* palms growing in masses in the water. These passages are full of crocodiles. As I sat in the canoe we passed so close to a very large one that I could have held out my hand and touched it. It did not move. I believe it was this crocodile that a few days later seized and carried off a little boy of seven, whom his mother was bathing in a shallow pool by the village. They come into the villages at night and prowl about the huts. I kept to my hut at night.

Each of the Islands has something specially worthy to be remembered—on Ugi it is a species of frog, the largest in the world—and on Gela surely the bird there described to Dr. Codrington: "There is a perpetual call resounding through the trees ... I am told it proceeds from a bird, of the shape and colour of a candle end, without wings, legs, tail or feathers, but with a mouth, and a mouth only. It never goes out of the hole in which it lives, which is not surprising, but it is (they say) certainly a bird, which may surprise one." It should beware of the Cheshire cat.

The people of Gela are all Christians. The population has remained about the same, five thousand, for many years. But in the old heathen days it was certainly much greater. About forty years ago the numbers

* The same name is given to this palm in parts of Indonesia.

in all the islands went down very rapidly because of the new diseases which the Europeans introduced. We used to discuss the population question at our synods. At one of these discussions a bachelor priest of great probity of life got up during a heated talk and said: "Well, all I can say is this, that wherever I have lived among the people the native population has gone up." He seemed astonished at our applause, but felt he had scored a point.

The people are said to be lazy. I have not found them so. Very often one man can give you a wrong impression of all his people. This happened to me at the beginning. One day while I was at Norfolk Island a cow became bogged, and the Archdeacon took a party of us to pull it out. A boy waded out into the swamp and tied a rope round its horns, and the rest of us lined up along the rope where the mud was shallow and prepared to pull. We all heaved with a will. Then suddenly the rope broke, and the Archdeacon and all of us fell flat in the mud—all but one boy, who remained standing, contemplating the rest of us. The Archdeacon was furious. Covered with mud, he rushed up to him, storming: "Why didn't you fall down? Why are you standing up clean?" This Gela boy smiled serenely. "It was because I wasn't pulling," he said. Somehow I got it into my head then that he stood for all Gela boys. But I was to find I was wrong; Daniel was the exception.

I had a different experience of Gela schoolboys when I was living for a time at a school for small boys on the island. After the Eucharist on my birthday, I went up the hill and had my breakfast, and the thirty or forty boys all gathered round my house, as I thought to give me birthday greetings. But when I came out they surrounded me, seized me and lifted me up on their shoulders and carried me down the hill, throwing water over me and pelting me with red mud which plastered me all over. They took me to the end of the wharf and threw me in the sea. It may be they had learnt this custom from boys who had been at Pawa school, where the custom prevails, though it is an old custom; Melanesians are very democratic and they used to do it from time to time to their chiefs. They say it is a mark of honour and affection, and of course, if it happens to you, you accept it as such. But it would certainly surprise headmasters at home, or the leaders of political parties, with whom Melanesians would find it natural to follow this old custom of theirs.

Twice in my time the Melanesians have struck out with new and original ideas. The first was the Melanesian Brotherhood, and the second when Willie Masuraa of Mala originated the "Church Association". The idea was that the Melanesian Church ought to be self-supporting, to pay its own clergy and catechists (which so far the European Mission had been doing), send out its own missionaries, build and staff its own schools and hospitals and generally speaking cease to rely on European help. He called his plan the Mala Church Association, and it was taken up and followed on Gela. They assessed every communicant so much a year and appointed several small committees for special purposes. They leased a considerable portion of native land and made a large farm. The Farm Committee found a man with a knowledge of proper farming and employed labourers, paid by the Association, who would thus learn good methods and then go back to their villages and use their knowledge to help to improve all the farms of the village people. The produce of the main farm would pay for all the work of the Gela church. There would be a School Committee to find sites for and build up boarding schools for boys and girls; there would be a Medical Committee who would establish Gela hospitals; a Missionary Committee to find men for the Retatasiu, the Missionary Brotherhood, and to send and support missionaries to New Guinea and beyond it; a Literature Committee to translate the Bible and other books and get them printed; finally there would be a Finance Committee to collect the assessment from all the communicants and keep the books. All these committees would work under the general supervision of the main committee, consisting of the President and the heads of the other committees. Anyone recovering from illness would give a thank offering. Masuraa added a "Band of Consolation", consisting of men who went to work on plantations or for the Government, who before they went made a vow in church to dedicate a fixed portion of their pay (a large portion) to the Association.

Under a very able Gela man, who had taken an honourable part as a sergeant in the Japanese war, this plan has been worked out on Gela. After a year the Gela church had a bank balance fifteen times larger than in previous years; and there was a flourishing central farm. The chief difficulty was to find anyone able to lead the Finance Committee and keep the books, but help came from a European layman. All European church members living on Gela were members of the Church Association, and partners in the work; but the native people were the leaders of the movement, it was their Association to be run by themselves for their own church. This is its beginning. How these Associations will succeed remains to be seen. It will depend on whether the Church can produce men and women capable of carrying them through. But it is a plan not suggested by Europeans, but coming from the native Christians themselves, and for this reason received by them with enthusiasm. They want to stand on their own feet.

There was a Melanesian priest named James Toganiande who though a native of Gela, went as a missionary to Guadalcanar and lived there for many years. Then when he was about sixty he became a leper and came home to his own island, and his people built him a leaf hut outside the village on a small grass hill, where he could live alone and not infect anyone in the village. His leprosy was becoming severe; but he was not content to spend his last years in idleness. He acquired a blackboard and some chalk, and every morning he came out of his hut and taught the people who sat on the slope below him, and then he would write notes of what he had been saying on the board. His fame spread, and people came from far villages to listen to this dying leper priest explaining more perfectly to them the way of the Christian life. I used to visit him there, and never was there anyone more cheerful than Father James even when the leprosy got very bad. He went on teaching as long as he was able. The people listened in the way people do listen when they come up against the real thing, someone in whom there is no pretence, but a deep belief in what he is saying; and moreover who talked in Melanesian way, with a thorough knowledge and understanding of the lives and the difficulties of those to whom he spoke, and not as a white man.

Gela was one of the first islands where the Government set up a native court with a native judge to try less serious cases. One question to be decided was about a girl who was to be married: who should get the bride price, her parents or the man who had adopted her when she was a baby, and fed and brought her up? Native custom was certainly in favour of the latter. An adopted child becomes in native opinion the real child of those who adopt her. I was one of the witnesses on this occasion. The trouble was that the native judge had members of his own clan in both parties, and it is very difficult to go against a clansman. He heard our side first and then he listened to the witnesses on the other side. At the end of the hearing he turned to us and complimented us on the way we had given our evidence. "You have," he said, "a very strong case, very strong indeed." Then he turned to the other side and said, "So have you, a very good case indeed". He paused a little and then ended, "I have no idea about the matter myself. The court is closed." So nothing was done, but in the end the two parties agreed to a compromise.

Another controversy almost caused a schism in the Gela church. The question was whether at the end of the Eucharist you should sing a single Alleluia or a sevenfold one. The villages were hotly divided. Most of the people on the smaller island of Gela were for the sevenfold form, while most on the larger island ridiculed it. They almost came to blows. At last one of the Gela priests who was respected by all of them said, "Let each village sing whichever kind it likes." All was well again. Other Christians might copy.

At one time there was a rather unusual newspaper on Gela, or at any rate it was circulated in an unusual way, edited and published by an enterprising District Officer and contributed to by the people of the island, besides containing news and official announcements. Each edition (there was only one copy) was carried from village to village by a Government policeman, who stood in the middle of the village and read the whole issue to the assembled people, like a town crier. As there are forty-two villages on the island, he got to know it all by heart before he had finished. It was, of course, written in the

Gela language, but it showed what a lot of English words were coming into that language in a slightly altered form.

It is not generally known that among Melanesians are poets who write poems in their own languages, and not merely dance songs. There was a poet on Gela who wrote a very beautiful poem (among others) on a waterfall. He also wrote most amusing verses, all in his own language, including a somewhat ribald poem about the deeds of an unpopular and rather foolish European District Officer, who annoyed the people, but they did not dare to say anything. At each village the D.O. visited, the people used to welcome him with a song—the words this poet had written—which of course he did not understand as he had never learned to speak their language; and this was just as well. After they had sung to him he used to thank them gravely for giving him such a splendid welcome. Thus the people felt they were getting their own back. He never knew; and he never thought of asking for a translation of the songs of welcome. They were not fit for it.

Gela is loyal to the British Government. It rejected Marching Rule, the first check this anti-British movement received. It even asked to pay double the tax the British Government imposed! And what could be more loyal than that? This was after the war. When the amount which the Government proposed was known the Gela people held an indignation meeting. "Does the Government esteem us so lightly? Could not the tax be increased? Why not double it? Surely it is a question of how much we can give, not how little." I was on the island at the time and heard what they said.

What struck me most on Gela was the way in which the people observed the Church festivals. There are about twenty large churches on Gela and each is dedicated to some saint, so that about twenty festivals are kept during the year. Each village keeps its own feast but many people come to it from other villages, by road or canoe, and take part in it. On the eve of the festival these people begin to arrive till perhaps there are five or six hundred of them. Then comes the first Evensong of the feast, and a procession is formed led by the cross bearer, the thurifer and some small boy (the boat boy) and the taperers with torches. Incense and torches are native made. These

The village of Sulufou. The long building to the left is the Melanesian Mission church

ARTIFICIAL ISLANDS IN TAE LAGOON, MALA

A lectern

EXAMPLES OF MELANESIAN ART

The carved figure of an angel used as a
lectern

A font

men will all be in scarlet cassocks and white cottas, also home made. Then come the village catechists, some twenty or thirty, in cassocks and surplices. The cassocks are home-made with what material can be got, so some are red, some blue, some green or other colours. It is a gay scene. Last come the clergy. The church is packed with the village people and their visitors, and there is barely room for the procession to move up to the altar. The Gela people are musical and the singing is beautiful; one of the visiting clergy preaches; the church is full of lights, also home-made. At the end of Evensong there is a preparation service for the Eucharist next morning. The rest of the evening and a part of the night is spent in the houses, hearing all the news of Gela from the visitors, who have come well supplied with food for the morrow, or singing Gela songs. But all are up next morning before it is light, having fasted from the evening before. They bathe and dress in their best to do honour to the King they are to meet.

Then comes the procession again, with last of all the Gela priest who is to celebrate the Eucharist, with his deacon and sub-deacon. The service is sung. There comes the moment of consecration and a great silence, not a sound from the hundreds of kneeling people. Then rank after rank they come up while hymns are sung softly, and four of the clergy pass along the ranks saying in their own tongue the words Christians have heard for so many centuries: "This is my Body which is given for you; this is my Blood which is shed for you." There is the final procession, and then a feast follows, and in small parties the visitors begin to go home. Gela has once more worshipped Christ the King and has been keeping the Communion of Saints, which my own country of New Zealand has so largely forgotten.

CHAPTER THIRTEEN

NORTH MALA

THE island of Mala is often called Malaita. But the latter is properly the name of about twelve miles of coast on the north-west corner of the island, the part first seen by the Spaniards in 1565, which led them to call the whole island by this name. Malaita apparently means "original Mala"; it may have been the site of the first settlers who came to the island. At the north end of Mala on the eastern side is Tae (east) lagoon, about thirty miles long and two or three miles wide, enclosed on the sea side by a coral reef through which are occasional openings. In this big lagoon are dotted about some fifty artificial islands, built up by the people with irregular blocks of coral, sometimes round an outstanding rock, sometimes merely in places where the water was fairly shallow. The oldest and largest, Sulufou, is only about two hundred yards long and not much more than fifty yards across, and had at one time about eight hundred people living on it. The houses were so close together that you had to walk sideways between the rows. The older lads live together in houses built at the edge of the island over the water; when you lie on your sleeping mat you hear the lapping of the water a few feet below you.

The people of these islands are the best fishermen in the Solomons, using great nets which they make themselves. They are all completely at home in the water, even the babies; you see tiny mites in miniature canoes two or three feet long paddling or poling themselves about with complete confidence. Parts of the lagoon are shallow and others deep; in the shallow parts the men in the canoes use twelve-foot poles and standing up in the canoe propel it rapidly and gracefully along; in the deep parts they sit down and use their paddles.

While I was living in Tae Lagoon among these islanders I saw an island being made. It took a man and his wife about six months to make one large enough for a leaf house for themselves and their children. They chose a spot where the water was about twelve feet deep and then made a raft of logs, which they towed with their canoe to where the bottom of the lagoon was rough coral. There Martin dived down with a crowbar and brought up jagged lumps to load on the raft, which was then towed back to the site of the future island. They only spent an occasional day at this work, but in six months had their island and house built and were living on it. Since then they have gone on enlarging it till it is now a good size. These people all go to the mainland daily, in canoes or swimming, to work their gardens and bring water and firewood to their islands. They are very healthy, vigorous folk. Of course an occasional exceptionally high spring tide may submerge some of the islands. Then they sit on their beds and say, "What bad tides we are having", as we speak about bad weather.

Dr. Ivens and Arthur Hopkins who both lived among these people, (the latter for years and the former for six months) have both written about them,* but neither described a custom that once flourished among the five thousand islanders: the custom of the *manu*. The word *manu* in their language means either a bird or epileptic. A boy was chosen and set apart to live alone in a house by himself for the rest of his life, and never marry. He was the *manu* and held in great respect, but as far as I know his only function was to keep the peace. When one island threatened war with another, the *manu* was sent to stop the war, and his office was so sacred and he himself held in such honour that, so they told me, it was unthinkable for any to disobey him. The last *manu* died a good many years ago and should have been replaced by some young boy chosen to succeed him, but I believe he never was. It seems to be one of those customs that the influence of Europeans has killed. There were certain signs by which the boy to succeed the *manu* was discovered. Whether the spirit of the dying *manu* entered into his successor I am not sure, but probably this was their belief. His

* *Isles of King Solomon*—Hopkins.
  Island Builders of the Pacific—Ivens.

special dress, like that of a Catholic priest—a garment like an alb, a stole, girdle and turban, all of native material—was dug up and shown to me. There seems to be a resemblance to the Dalai Lama, but the manu was only a peacemaker, not a ruler.

The first missionary of our Church to go to these islands was Arthur Hopkins, a very small man, physically weak, but a good Cambridge scholar. This was in 1902 when that part of Mala was really wild and savage, more so than anywhere else in Melanesia. He was my chief friend during all the thirty years we were both members of the Mission. He lived partly in these artificial islands and partly at Fiu, across the island—another wild part—but it was when we spent a year together at Norfolk Island that I came to know him best.

In those days Hopkins owned a gig and (which was like him) an excitable and wild horse to draw it; and he and I used to drive out on Saturdays to Mt. Pitt and picnic there, Hopkins always taking the reins though he was no driver. One day we set off from our gates at full gallop, the near wheel going over the deep four-foot ditch beside the road. Hopkins turned to me with a placid smile, saying, "That was because I pulled the wrong rein!" It was always exciting driving with Hopkins. Another day we went at a hard gallop down a steep hill while he discussed philosophy, one hand on the reins. Another time after we had our picnic we had to set about harnessing our skittish horse. The boys usually did this and Hopkins had very vague ideas about it. However he seized the breeching and standing right behind the horse began to shove it hard under the animal's tail. "Seems very stiff today!" he said to me anxiously. The reason was that he had not noticed some brambles that had got fastened to the breeching, and it was the brambles that he was thrusting vigorously under the tail, while the horse looked round at him with a kindly smile.

That was Hopkins, physically one of the smallest and weakest of men, quite unpractical, mentally and spiritually very great, the bravest man I have known. We thought there were probably several guardian angels allotted to him.

When he first went to Mala there was only a handful of Christians,

"kanakas"* i.e. Mala men returned from working on sugar plantations in Australia. They built a high stockade round their houses and
had a sentry armed with a gun always on watch. In this stockade
Hopkins lived. Many attempts were made on his life by Mala *ramo*,
killers who killed anyone for money. He had a Gela missionary
with him who was shot and killed in the next house to his. On
another occasion when sitting on his verandah with a friend, a party
of *ramo* walked up and shot his friend, the blood splashing on
Hopkins. He jumped up, seized his pigeon gun and fired at the
ramo as they ran. "I did not think I should hit them," he said to me,
"because I had never fired a gun before and because I had my eyes
shut, but I thought I *ought* to do it." He was the mildest of men.

On one occasion he was told that, if he went along the coast in his
whaleboat, he would be killed as he went past a certain village. Of
course he went. As he came opposite this village two large canoes full
of armed men dashed out and made for the boat. "All right," he said
to his crew, "row hard!" and turned the boat straight for the canoes.
Much puzzled the canoes turned away and as they turned Hopkins
followed them round. Nervously they made a dash for the shore.

Once again he came to a village and they told him they had
decided to kill him. "Very well," he said, "but wait a minute, I have
something for you," and pulled out some sticks of tobacco and
passed them round. They decided not to kill the goose with the
golden eggs. He had innumerable adventures of this sort, but went
on quietly, year after year, steadily building up a Christian church
among those very wild people.

When I first went to Fiu we bathed in the river with armed sentries
walking up and down guarding us; and the same was done when the
Christians met for their prayers. Some were killed by the heathen.
Years later when I was living there it was a large Christian village of
five hundred people, two long lines of thatched houses along the
coral shore.

One dark night as I was sitting in my house the village catechist
came to tell me that a man in the village had run amok and was

---

* *Kanaka* is the Hawaiian word for the Maori *Tangata* and means "a man". The first
kanakas went to work in South America, from Hawaii.

chasing people with an axe. The catechist seemed disturbed. I took a lantern and walked along down the village but saw no sign of anyone till we came near the end of it after five hundred yards of houses. Then my companion whispered, "He is in there," pointing to a house. I went in with my lantern and there he was, standing on a low platform, a tall lean naked fellow, muttering to himself and fingering a very bright, sharp axe. The catechist hovered about outside. I was uncertain how one proceeds on such occasions, so I asked him if he would like a cup of tea. He stopped muttering and looked down at me and said yes, so I called to the catechist to go to my house and get one.

It seemed a long time before he came back, while I talked about anything I could think of. At last the tea came and I went out and brought it in and gave it, but the man wouldn't let go the axe. He was convinced that everyone wanted to kill him. "Well," I said, at last, "come along to my house, you'll be safe there". He agreed but still said he must take the axe, so we walked along together, I with my lantern, he with his axe. You could feel people about, but could see no one. I took him into my study, locked the door from the inside and put the key in my pocket, to make sure he could not get out at anyone, and then gave him short Evensong and two aspirins, and we spent the night together. He would not give up the axe. People prowled round all night, which annoyed me as I thought they would excite him, but they told me they were afraid for me. They also sent for Government police five miles away, who arrived at dawn. I managed to get the axe from him and brought him out to them. He recovered in the end. It is difficult to know the right treatment in these cases. I hope medical opinion approves of mine.

CHAPTER FOURTEEN

THE WAR

I THOUGHT in 1939, after a visit to England, that I was going back to the quietest spot in the world, where the war would not touch us. Like most people I had no prevision of the coming of the Japanese to the Solomons. However some people seem to have thought of it, for the British Government in sending out a Resident Commissioner several years before, had warned him that some day the Japanese might reach this far. I knew they had, in the peace years, acquired plenty of information about our harbours. Years before when I was living on San Cristoval on the weather coast, where Europeans did not go, a Japanese ship had come into the harbour taking soundings. They told me they had come to sell the people bananas! I duly reported this to the Government.

The remarkable thing about the coming of the Japanese was the rapidity of it. We heard of Pearl Harbour, and then it seemed a very short time before we heard of the fall of Singapore; then the Japanese advance through Indonesia and finally their arrival at Rabaul in New Britain, not far from us. Nothing seemed to stop them long. All that seemed to happen very quickly, and people began to think of leaving the Islands. But when the Japanese reached Rabaul they stayed there for some time, consolidating before coming on. They thought they had plenty of time. Had they come on then, they would probably have got to Fiji and New Zealand, for the Americans at that time, after the disaster at Pearl Harbour, were not ready to stop them.

When they did advance they came on again very rapidly. I was living in the Tae Lagoon near the north end of Mala, as one of a Household of the Melanesian Brotherhood. By that time most of the white people had left the Islands. There was a great deal of panic in their going. The last steamers to leave were crammed, and luggage was left on the wharves. The Melanesians could not help noticing it, and there was a good deal of looting, for which the people were punished a few years later. It was a time of confusion and made a deep impression on the Solomon Islanders who saw it all.

When the Japanese came close and began to bomb us, our Bishop, who was living a few miles from the capital at Tulagi, told us all we could either leave or remain, whichever we liked, but if we remained and the Japanese invaded the Group, we were not to throw ourselves in their way, but to retire to the hills. He said he did not want any martyrs if he could help it. Almost all the members of the Mission remained, even the women. So did the Roman Catholic missionaries and some members of the South Sea Evangelical Mission. One of us who stayed was a very brave lady, Mrs. Emily Sprott, living on Ysabel, where the people took her up into the hills and hid her in a smoky leaf house and fed her on taro. For her conduct in the war she received the M.B.E. Sister Stead, head of our Mothercraft School, retired to the hills on Mala.

Bishop Baddeley, who in the 1914-18 war had been a colonel in the fierce fighting in France, and won the D.S.O. and M.C., both with bar, played a fine part in the Solomon Island War. The Government, I believe, were intending to carry out orders and retire to Fiji, but the Bishop felt that it would make a great difference to the people if the Government remained, and his courage and encouragement helped them to decide to do so. Some of the District Officers did splendid work in the months that followed; the Resident Commissioner himself went to the hills on Mala. The Bishop remained at the Mission headquarters on Gela, till he saw Tulagi four miles away going up in flames; and was the last European to leave, going by night in a small launch across to Mala through a very rough sea, but thinking not of the sea but of the numerous Japanese warships then prowling about. He got over safely and took to the hills where he tramped about for some months encouraging the people and keeping in touch with us when it was possible. Then when the Americans came in he returned to Gela, and finding the Japanese had destroyed his house, he built a leaf hut and called it his palace. That was by then an American station and he kept open house for them. The Americans had a great admiration for him and said he should have been a general. He was decorated by them after the war. It was he, more than any other, who kept the British name bright in the eyes of the people, and he was the central figure of the war in their estimation. After he got back to Gela he sent me a letter to come over to him—a short note, but he said he was tired, having been sitting in a trench with a Roman Catholic priest till 2 a.m., "condition red". I did not then know what that meant, and took it to my neighbour, a South Sea Evangelical missionary. He was very grave about it and shook his head: "Whisky, I'm afraid", he said, "till 2 a.m.!" "Condition red" meant that the Japanese were bombing them, as I learnt myself later when I too went over to Gela.

The Roman Catholic missionaries remained and proved themselves brave men and women. Some were murdered by the Japanese. The planters and traders also played a fine part in the war. Some who went out returned again to guide the Americans, and then became Coast Watchers. Their deeds have been celebrated and they played a real part in winning the war in the Solomons, and must have saved hundreds of American lives. If they had not been very successful as planters, they came into their own in the fighting and made a name for themselves.

When the Japanese came in, burnt Tulagi, overran Gela and seized on Guadalcanar, the Government looked about for people to report their movements, numbers, and so on, which could then be passed on to the Americans to help them when they should come. There were so few white men left in the Group that I naturally volunteered for the job and was duly appointed a Coast Watcher, and given a formal written commission—"to help you if the enemy capture you", I was told, though I knew it would not have done that. My job was to send anything I could get hold of from the northern end of Mala; but I was a very inferior sort of Coast Watcher as I had no tele-radio, there were not enough to go round, and I had to send my messages by runners across a range of hills two thousand feet high, of course far too slow a method.

I wanted to send them by drums. In Arosi I had often sent messages seventy miles by drums, the people picking them up in village after village and passing them on. It only took twenty minutes to send a message fifty miles; I had it all arranged, with the different villages eight miles apart all ready; but the man at the other end had never seen this method and did not think it would be accurate, so after all I had to trust to runners, who took a day to do the thirty miles over the hills.

One moonlight night we saw a Japanese fleet anchor near us for several hours (on their way to Guadalcanar). About the same time a landing was made fifteen miles along our coast and a Japanese camp established. One of my boys went there and back in an afternoon, counted the Japanese, noted where their guns were posted and sold them bananas. I passed on the news of this, and it reached the other side of the island in time, but was not believed, and both the District Officer and the doctor at our hospital were nearly caught. The enemy arrived at 4 a.m. at the hospital and the doctor dashed up the hill behind in his pyjamas. The Japanese took his surgical instruments but did no other harm. The District Officer was sitting down to an early breakfast when the enemy arrived. He had managed to get a ham—a rare treat—but left it hastily and hid. The Japanese ate his ham. After that he was heart and soul in the war against them. He was a very good District Officer, killed later in a plane.

Japanese planes were continually passing over us, and one day one came down nearby. We sent word over and Government police came across and captured the crew, though they tried to commit suicide. Another time we rescued some American airmen. They were from a carrier and had lost it twenty miles off Santa Ana, about two hundred miles from us. They had drifted that distance for nine days in their rubber dinghy, with very little food, but plenty of water because the weather was rough, with rain storms. They had shot at a following shark and made a hole in their rubber boat, and it had capsized several times. At last they got to our reef, but, not knowing of any opening, they came over the top through the thundering surf, and were bruised on the coral. The islanders thought they were Japanese and ran out with spears; while the Americans thought the natives were cannibals and prepared to fight it out. I had them with me for some days, healing their sores and feeding them with taro, all I had myself; and then sent word over and a plane came and took them away.

It was all a time of confusion, with wild rumours flying about, and the truth impossible to discover. For the first time for years I saw every Melanesian armed again as in the old days. People went about in companies, as it was not safe to go alone; in two weeks there were half a dozen murders near where I was, people cut up on the roads just because everyone's nerves were on edge. Patrols of Japanese came along sometimes. The first time the rumour of this reached me I went up into the hills to stay with a friendly chief. It was wild weather but he turned me out because he said the Japanese might not want him to help me, and down I came again in the rain. The people had dug a hole and buried my books in the ground to save them from the enemy patrol, but as it was raining continuously they were not worth digging up again. Most of my books I had left on Gela, about five hundred, language books I could never replace. These were all torn up and burnt by the Japanese.

The loyal islanders were bribed with offers of goods to give me up, but this only amused them. You did not know what might happen to you if you were caught; it might be a concentration camp, or perhaps a prison ship, as happened to one of our missionaries; or death at once as happened to another, John Barge, who was one of our best men, everyone's friend, and adored by the Melanesians. His station was inland in New Britain, and there he remained for some two years, and at last came down to the shore, hoping, I suppose, to hear some news. He was seized, tied up and beheaded, and the body left for his boys to bury. They may have thought him a spy, but he had done nothing worthy of death.

After some eight months the Japanese at the camp on Mala were all killed by the Americans. There were then only some fifty in the camp. The Americans landed at our hospital thirty miles away and the Melanesians cut tracks for them through the forest so that they were able to surround the camp by night and place machine guns in position. In the morning the Japanese sat down to breakfast in the open at trestle tables, and soon there was just a mass of smashed tables and utensils and dead or wounded men. About five hundred heathen hillmen were at the back of the Americans and rushed in to collect the blood of the dead and dying Japanese to sacrifice to the spirits. A few Japanese escaped and were hunted down and shot by the Mala men as they tried to swim out to sea. That day I met parties of excited natives running along wearing the clothes of the dead Japanese. They were seeing how white men wage war.

The Melanesians did not like the Japanese. At first they dealt fairly and even paid for the fowls and ducks they took, but they let it be known that when things settled down, the people would have to work for them without pay. They had no idea they would lose the Islands again. They prepared for civil government and circulated Solomon Island notes with a Japanese stamp across them (I forget the exact words). But as they began to be driven out they shot at sight natives they saw on the roads. Even before that when they came to a village and wanted a coconut they would point to the tree with a gun and then turn the gun on one of the villagers. The meaning of this gesture was unmistakable: "Climb up and get me a nut". The natives, needless to say, thought this bad manners. Then anyone who was travelling on the roads or by canoe, was searched by the Japanese for letters. They did not like this either. Moreover the Japanese could not talk pidgin English, and the Melanesians therefore considered them uneducated and barbarians. Also the Melanesians liked the Chinese traders, of whom there were a good many in the Group, and whom the Japanese massacred wherever they found them.

When the Americans came in the first fierce fighting was on Gela, and Guadalcanar. On Gela many of the Japanese, driven off Gavutu Island, swam to the mainland, threw away their weapons, and fled across the hills, where they were hunted down and killed. Even three years after the war, a Gela native pig hunting found a solitary Japanese dying in the forest, after living all that time alone on roots. The main fighting was on Guadalcanar, where for some time it was touch and go, but gradually the Japanese, for the first time in that war, were stopped, held, and at last turned back. It was one of the turning points in the war. Off Savo Island, eight miles from

Guadalcanar, there was a naval battle, one that we lost; and our Melanesian priest there told me that hundreds of bodies were washed ashore, locked together friend and foe. There were so many it was hard for him to bury them, but he did try to read the burial service over all the Americans; the Japanese he pushed off into the sea. Yet some of them also were Christians. At Siota a Japanese officer told our lads that he was an Anglican Christian and his name was Andrew; they saw him go into the Cathedral and pray there. Next day he was killed by the Americans.

On Guadalcanar our boys' school at Maravovo was completely destroyed by the Japanese, who used the lovely chapel as a toilet, and made Maravovo the headquarters of one of their generals. The headmaster and his assistant and a party of boys made their way forty miles to the Americans at Lungga, though the country was full of enemy soldiers, and they often had to hide in the long grass to avoid them. Only one of the party was shot; the rest made their way in the dark through the American wire without being seen by the sentries. At Tabalia the chapel of the Native Brotherhood was burnt and the Brotherhood headquarters destroyed.

The Melanesians soon formed a great liking for the Americans, especially for the Marines, who came first, and whom they called *na vure tambu*, the holy people, because, the Gela people said, they were fierce fighters, lived hard, never stole anything from the villages, and the Gela women were as safe with them as they were with their own people. But they liked all the Americans. It was not only their lavish generosity that won their hearts. The Americans showed almost no colour feeling. This may sound surprising and is not, I suppose, true in their own country. Perhaps they felt they were far from home and would never have any close relations with Solomon Islanders. Still, this fact, and their great friendliness, surprised and delighted the Melanesians. They invited the Islanders into their mess to eat with them, and in Melanesia to eat together is the great test of friendship. They had not found this with others.

The Americans in their turn liked the Solomon Islanders, who to their great surprise proved to be Christians and not cannibals. They saw the Islanders filling their village churches every day, even during the Japanese occupation, when the women and children used to live in the hills. Every morning before the Japanese were about they came down to church, said their prayers, and then retired to the hills again. Wounded or escaping Americans always found help and succour in the villages. The Islanders appreciated the friendship they found in the Americans. And it was the Americans, not the British, who had saved them from the Japanese. It was not easy to explain to people who knew so little of the world that the British and Americans were partners, and the British busy elsewhere. They wanted the Americans to take over the Islands after the war. Many of the Americans were strong anti-imperialists and anti-British; a few were Communists and tried to sow the seeds of Communism, but had not time to do much more than urge the people to be "against the government", and in particular against the British Government after the war.

I lived with the Americans at their anti-aircraft school at Siota for six months. They were the friendliest of people and for me it was a very happy time, and made me permanently pro-American.

Above all, the Melanesians liked the British. It would be idle to say the British Government had always been loved or always a good one, but it had been getting steadily better and had given the people a fair deal, and all through the war the people, with hardly an exception, were thoroughly loyal and gave a great deal of help. And in spite of the nationalist movement after the war, the feeling for the post-war British Government is a warm one. Certainly throughout the war the people were pro-British.

CHAPTER FIFTEEN

MARCHING RULE

THE war was a time of great confusion and unsettlement in the minds of the Melanesians. The impotence of the British against the Japanese, the might of the Americans, the vast power of the weapons of war, all made a deep impression on them, and prepared the way for the nationalist movement called Marching Rule which followed hard on the heels of the war. Compared with other places the Solomons suffered little, nor did we have a hard time. We were only on the fringe of the real stuff and its horrors and heroism, we were only sailing through the edge of a cyclone. But with the war, all the same, a change came over the Solomons. We could not have over a hundred thousand visitors and remain the same as before.

At the end of the war I was living on Mala, and soon I heard that a new thing had appeared among the Mala people. They called it *Masinga Lo* or *Masinga Rulu*. The meaning of the first word nobody knew. White people soon corrupted the words into Marching Rule. It no doubt meant Marx's Law or Marx's Rule. But the very fact that the meaning of the word was unknown made it more mysterious and attractive. It began on Mala and probably through the influence of some American Communists; certainly the people believed that Americans were the authors of it. Many Americans had been anti-British and very critical of colonialism, and had talked about it to the Melanesians, who listened because they liked and admired the Americans so much. It seemed to the people that the Americans must have a tremendous amount of that *mana*, spiritual power, which shows itself in strength, efficiency and success. Nearly everyone on Mala hurried to join the new movement. The entrance fee was one American dollar, or five cents for a baby. You could not join with British or native money.

There were some remarkable things about the movement, and one was the way in which it was organised. Those who knew Melanesia and had lived long in the Solomons were amazed at the rapid way in which the movement spread and the excellence of the organisation in the whole of Mala from village to village, and then across the sea to Ulawa and San Cristoval till it passed on to Guadalcanar, tried to get into Gela, and got a firm footing in Ysabel. There it ended. It did not, I think, reach the western Solomons, New Georgia, and the other islands of that Group. But Mala has a large proportion of the total population of the Group and they are the most virile people. It seemed that before long all the Solomon Islanders would become Marching Rule. In the islands which it reached ninety-five per cent of the people joined it.

It was also most remarkable how it united all the people. Before the war no one could have believed this possible. In 1926, Mr. Bell, the District Officer on Mala, with his Assistant and twenty native police, had been murdered at Sinaranggu, when trying to impose for the first time a poll tax on the hill people. The acting Resident Commissioner had panicked, pulled down the British flag on Mala, and appealed to Australia for help to suppress a general rising of the Solomon Islanders! Europeans living in the Group knew what nonsense this was; the Solomon Islanders were then incapable of anything of that sort. Most of the people of Mala prepared to fight the Sinaranggu people, for it was only a local disturbance. Deep differences in language, in custom, in government divided the people of the different islands. The inhabitants of one island were foreigners to those of another, and used to be killed at sight. There were then no common leaders. Yet here in Marching Rule was something uniting them all. Those who joined said: "Now we are all one." It seemed incredible. It astonished those of us who knew them best. I talked to a native of North Mala and asked him why he had joined and why he liked Marching Rule. He said, "Because it has made us Melanesians all one. We are all brothers now. Before it began if I had tried to walk to South Mala through the central districts of Koio and Areare I should have been killed long before I got to South Mala. But now the Koio and Areare people say to us, 'Come through when you wish, we are all one'." And the same thing was said to me on San Cristoval, many of whose people are hereditary enemies of Mala men. "But now," they said to me, "we are all one with the Mala people." And so it was too in the other islands. British rule had not united them, Christianity had not united them, and here they were suddenly swept into a unity never dreamed of before by this new movement for independence and self government. It amazed us all.

These were perhaps the three most remarkable things about the movement: its surprisingly excellent organisation, the amazing speed with which it spread, and the unity which it gave to a hitherto deeply divided people. There was a certain amount of Communism in it. The leaders told the members to give up their individual farms, to which they were so much attached, and to make large communal ones instead, an idea quite foreign to them, but they did it. Europeans were forbidden to enter these farms, but I saw some and they were very large. They were a failure. The people could not be got to work on them, for each loved his own farm too much. Food ran short, and famine followed. The communal farms were soon given up and the old order was followed again, and that was the end of Communism in the movement.

It was very hard to find out the facts about Marching Rule. No European must be told anything about it. Men you had known from their childhood, who you expected would tell you anything, would not tell you a word about it. The organisation was very complete.

It had various chiefs, some over the whole, some over villages only. It had its own guards and police. Women took a prominent part in it; they were put in charge of the communal farms. It was pro-American and anti-British. Their slogan was, "All the British to leave the Islands". They wanted the Americans to come back. An easy explanation for this was that they expected to get a lot of goods from them. The Americans during the war had been very generous; I was told by a man who knew the Mala people as none other did that the Americans left £100,000 of American money on Mala. And it is true that the Marching Rule commanded what they called "custom houses" to be built in every village of the coast. These were

I

tall towers built of leaf, two or three stories high, which the Government supposed to be watch towers to warn the village of the approach of police. They were in fact simply copies of a tall leaf house which the Americans had built at Tulagi as a customs house. But the Government had not seen this American tower in the war, and thought the copies of it in the villages something mysterious and hostile. Government police destroyed them.

But Marching Rule was something much more deeply rooted than a desire for American goods. The people liked the Americans, and they expected them to come back and give them independence. The Americans fostered this idea by leaving parties with planes behind for many months after the war. Marching Rule might not have flourished if they had not done this. As it was, for a long time there were the most fantastic stories of the arrival of the Americans; their footmarks were seen on the beaches; they were living in caves in the interior; all sorts of proofs were offered that they had come back, and the rumours were believed everywhere by a credulous people; it was impossible to shake their belief that the Americans were either showing themselves openly or about to do so. Letters supposed to be written by Americans were passed from hand to hand. And with the coming of the Americans the Solomon Islanders would be given at once self-government and independence. Many Americans had told them so.

Though friends of Britain, many of the Americans were very critical of what they called British Imperialism, and they talked a lot of nonsense about it, and of what they thought was the wickedness of it, to the Solomon Islanders. They had no idea what a lot of good things the British Government had done for the people. It struck me that the Americans in the war were far more illiterate and uneducated than the New Zealanders who fought in the Solomons. They themselves told me this was because so many of them came from what we in New Zealand call "back blocks", out-of-the-way parts of that great country. I don't know if this was true. But that may have been the reason why most of them knew so little of the world outside America.

At the beginning of the movement the people on Mala built

stockades round their villages. Sometimes these were poor affairs, but sometimes they were strong ones, with big gates barred and padlocked to keep out the British. I visited one of these and when I appeared a sentry rushed to the gate, unlocked it and threw it open for me. I went in and talked to the people and when I came back the sentry unlocked the gates again to let me out.

Marching Rule members refused to work for white people so there was for some time no labour for the plantations, which depend chiefly on Mala men. Only a few villages refused to join the movement, one being the village of Sulufou of nearly eight hundred people living on an artificial island in the Tae lagoon. None of the Melanesian priests of the Mission joined it, and so they were persecuted, ostracised, sent to Coventry, and had their goods stolen with impunity. They had a very hard time.

At first the Government thought they could use Marching Rule as an education for self government, but finding this impossible they reversed their policy, the leaders were imprisoned, and the movement went underground with fresh leaders whose names were kept secret. The people took to passive resistance, refused to pay taxes, refused to obey all orders of the Government and went quietly to gaol, about two thousand of them; in some villages only the women remained. The Government hoped that the women, left to do all the heavy work the men usually did, would persuade their men-folk to give in; it was not realised that the women were in the movement as strongly as the men. Passive resistance is difficult to overcome.

Sometimes it was active. I saw some Government police beaten up rather badly after visiting a Marching Rule village, and there was another occasion when a District Officer, threatened by a large and hostile crowd of armed men, had to retreat with his police into the sea. An old and loyal sergeant of police told me that the movement would not end till blood was shed; there was real danger of Europeans being murdered by heathen, if not by Christian, members of Marching Rule. The movement had much in common with the later troubles in Nyasaland, though with less violence, more passive resistance and of course on a smaller scale.

Except for the hostility to our clergy, Marching Rule was not at all anti-Christian. They all went to church just as before though some left the Anglican Church to join the Roman Church, because they had been told by the Melanesian Roman Church teachers that the Americans were all Roman Catholics and would impose that form of Christianity on all the people when they returned. This belief was generally held in the days of Marching Rule and caused uneasiness to members of other Christian communions. Melanesians will easily believe anything of this sort. I did not notice that European Roman Catholics denied the story, though they did not initiate it.

Soon after I moved to Gela, Marching Rule reached that island. The leaders burned with zeal to spread it, they were fanatics who could not be reasoned with. One of them came to Gela and went from village to village. He gathered the people into the churches, preaching fervently, mentioning that the British were referred to in the Bible as wolves clothed in sheep's clothing. He went thus through some twenty villages, and all the people in every village but one (Belaga) joined the movement. But Marching Rule was really impossible for Christians because it preached hate for all who did not belong to it. A week later I followed this fanatic through the same villages, taking two Gela friends with me, and all the people who had joined left it again, though they did not get back their dollars. That was the end of Marching Rule on Gela; it never got a footing again, and the refusal of Gela to join it had a good deal of influence.

Both the Government and our Mission showed weakness in dealing with Marching Rule because neither could quite make up its mind about it. The Government vacillated. First it encouraged it, then when things began to look very serious it tried to kill it by stern measures. When these had no effect it looked about for some other way. I had an idea when I was living on Mala of starting another society to be called Patana (Partner). In its native dress the word looked mysterious, like Masinga, and therefore attractive to Melanesians, but it meant partnership between British and Melanesians, which thousands of them really wanted. Very many did not want to join Marching Rule but they were intimidated, and so they followed the crowd. A large number urged me to set Patana going and promised to join. But the Resident Commissioner, who at that time was out to kill Marching Rule by putting, if need be, the whole population in gaol, asked me to give up Patana. So I did. Partnership is however the only real solution.

After the war new men came into the Government with new ideas. I did not see this stage of the dealings with Marching Rule because I was away on furlough, but when I came back after a year there was a great change. The Government had established Native Councils in each island. Each had its President and officers. The native council governed the island, taxed the people, had its own courts, established schools, all with the advice, and as regards final decisions with the consent, of British District Commissioners; in fact a mild form of self government. Marching Rule was not dead, it might flare up again, but the general atmosphere had changed from one of hostility to all Europeans to one of toleration and a much greater friendliness. The Government was much stronger; the District Commissioners and District Officers were wise and able men.

As to the future, no one can tell. The people still want to rule themselves and to be free of the British. They look wistfully to the past and would like to go back to their old way of life. The present generation has no idea what that way of life was like; they would not want to go back to it if they knew. There can be no return. Nor can they be isolated; new inventions have made the world one, and the Solomons are part of this larger world. They still need far more knowledge, especially medical and agricultural knowledge, and far more education in government, before they can hope to be independent.

The Melanesians were originally one of the most democratic peoples in the world, but it was village democracy. The whole village met together with the chief to discuss everything. When the chief saw what the majority wished he suggested that as the best thing; but it was the men of ability who carried weight in deciding. Of representative democracy, where the opinions of the more able carry no more weight in the final decision than the opinions of the ignorant, the people have no experience.

The chief drawback to British rule is the colour feeling of the British race. It is clean contrary to the teaching of the Christian faith but it is found in Christian missionaries as well as in Government officials. Some time ago there was a bishop, not of the present time, who would have said he had no colour feeling, but a very good and very loyal native priest who was talking to me one day said: "When an English priest goes to see the Bishop he finds him perhaps standing at the top of the steps of his verandah, and as soon as the Bishop sees him he says, 'Come in, old chap, and have a cup of tea.' But if I, or another Melanesian priest, goes to see him he stands at the top of the steps and says, 'Well, what have you come here for?' " It hurts.

When we have a sense of race superiority we hurt in a hundred ways without ever knowing we are doing so. Some despise the Melanesians, calling them "niggers" or "natives"—and the two words are now generally almost synonymous—or else condescending to them, which is even more galling, calling them a "child race" and treating them as children, adding often, "spare the rod and spoil the child". Both attitudes are quite different from friendship. Your friend may differ from you, in ability, in knowledge, in character, but there is equality in friendship nevertheless, and this is what we ought to give other races. It is not easy because the Melanesian's background is so different from ours. But it can be done, and the more easily if you know his language and his way of life; and it is the only thing he cares about. All Melanesians say the British have given them justice. I never heard any say we have given them friendship. It would not be amiss to substitute the modern word "friendship" for the old word "charity" in St. Paul's famous letter. Most people mean by that "benevolence", in some form or other, but friendship is deeper than that; and it is the word Christ himself gave us: "I call you no longer servants, but I have called you friends." Most Englishmen believe in their hearts that they are superior to the men of all other races. So long as this feeling lasts other races will give and feel respect indeed, but not friendship.

Marching Rule was the result of the great upheaval of the war. I hope "Patana" will carry the day. It may not do so if British officials stay in the islands only a short time as at present and therefore cannot hope to know and understand the people. What is really needed is men who are willing to give their lives to this work.

CHAPTER SIXTEEN

INFLUENCE OF EUROPEANS

THE coming of the British has influenced the Melanesians, including those in the Solomons, as much as the coming of the Austronesians influenced the Negritoes long ago [see Appendix]. It is giving them one language (English) as the Austronesians did, and changing their customs and way of life. History is repeating itself—with variations.

All Europeans have helped to break down the old society, though they have also brought a new unity; and the missionary has done this more than all others because he has given them a new religion in exchange for the old beliefs which entered into every part of the life of their former society. They ceased to dance when dancing was no longer dramatic prayer to the spirits in whom they had ceased to believe. At any rate the life left their dancing and it became a shadow of what it had been. In all sorts of ways, when they became Christians the old way of life broke down.

For example at a meeting of the Church Synod it was decided to regulate marriage by the Table of Affinity, which though not part of the Anglican prayer book is an appendix to it, drawn up from a study of the law of Moses. This meant in practice that young men could now marry women whom their own clan laws forbid them to marry, and to the Melanesians such marriages were regarded in the same way as we regard incest. The young men were triumphant, the older people bitter and unhappy. As a matter of fact their clan regulations were quite sufficient to forbid the marriage of near relations; technically by their rules some such marriages were possible, for example there was nothing in the clan rules to stop a girl marrying her father, since he and she were of different clans; but in practice these possible marriages never did take place. The clan rules regarding marriage were good. Yet no one in the Synod, except myself, seemed to think they ought to be kept. The law of Moses must be sacrosanct and binding on all Christians. But as soon as the people understood that the clan laws could now be broken, by consent of the Church, they began to pay less regard to the clan itself. And yet the whole structure of native society was bound up with the clan: the tenure of land, mutual help and hospitality of clansmen and many other things. The Church leaders did not realise that they might be causing a general breaking down of Melanesian society, which is so close-knit and so bound up in everything with the old religion, that if you touch one thing you bring about all sorts of unexpected and unforseen changes in other things.

But it is a great mistake to speak of Melanesian customs; the customs and the languages are different in each island, and in most of the islands they have never been studied. Bishop Patteson spoke some twenty Melanesian languages and was a master of eight of them. I am a philologist rather than a linguist, and though I have tried to preach in six or seven I never spoke more than three at all well. Most Europeans trust to interpreters, but they are often broken reeds and interpreting some speakers is very difficult. One of our bishops once got a catechist to interpret for him into the Raga language, while he preached in Mota. The catechist gave it up after the first sentence which he found beyond him, so he preached an entirely different sermon of his own in Raga, sentence by sentence. I never had the heart to tell the Bishop as I tried to listen to both sermons, both quite good; but it was a little confusing. Once at Tikopia the Bishop had with him an archdeacon from New Zealand and his Maori priest. The Maori preached in his own language, which the Archdeacon put into English, which the Bishop put into Mota, which the catechist put into Tikopian. I wonder what came out? It is very hard to translate a difficult English sentence suddenly. I was once faced with the sentence: "Of course, marriage is a social contract"—not easy to put into Mota. On another occasion a young priest for whom I was translating began by remarking: "This was a psychological moment in the history of Israel"! Like other things, interpreting needs practice and training. It is often bad in Government courts.

No Government officer has ever learnt a local language. This is partly the result of the policy of the British Government never to leave an officer for long on one island; nor even for very long in the Group. Thus the Government officer has had more excuse than the missionary for failing to understand the thought and way of life of the people. He has done what he could through the medium of pidgin English, but very few have come to know much about the people, certainly nothing like as much as, for example, the Roman Catholic missionaries, the best linguists in the Group.

The Government officials never realised who were the real chiefs. In appointing headmen they chose those who knew the most pidgin English, sometimes rogues who persuaded the official they were chiefs, while the proper chiefs were ignored. This certainly happened fairly often. Also the power of the real chiefs declined for other reasons. When a European District Officer set up his station and court in one of the islands all the cases of misconduct, at any rate all serious ones, had to go to him. Before that the village chief had judged them and fined the offenders. He knew much better than the District Officer the truth about the matter. With the fines he imposed he became the richest man in the village and gave lavish hospitality. Now he could no longer do this and became a person of no importance and his word had no weight. After the coming of the District Officer the individual villages were far worse governed than before.

Many of the laws imposed showed a lack of understanding. It seemed to the Government officers that there were far too many dogs in the villages and in the houses—and indeed so there were. A dog tax was imposed, which was more than the people could pay, so the police were sent to shoot all the dogs. But the dogs were for pig hunting and when they were shot numbers of wild pigs from the hills destroyed the village gardens.

Another law made it necessary for a native visiting a friend in another island to go first to the District Officer and buy a pass for a shilling. This meant hardship in some cases. A man might have to walk sixty miles each way and pay a shilling to visit a friend six miles away; not that this happened often, but the law caused irritation. A law was proposed forbidding Melanesians to wear anything more than a loin-cloth, and prohibiting European dress. The Bishop protested about this and the proposal was dropped, but the Melanesians had felt sore about it.

New ideas, new laws, came too many and too fast, even when they were good. The people were bewildered, always wondering what might come next; and they were never, of course, consulted. For instance, it could never have been understood by Melanesians that when they sold land they had lost it for ever. Everything returned in the next generation. When peace was made between two villages and an indemnity paid, the children of the victors paid back the indemnity to the children of the vanquished. So also with land, debts, and everything else. It would never enter their minds that something could be lost in perpetuity.

Taxes were another mystery, and Government officers had a hard job explaining the reason for them. One of them was explaining to a group of Melanesians that the taxes were paid so that the Solomon Islands could be protected by the British. "Otherwise," he said, "the Germans or the Japanese (this was long before the war) would come in and treat you far worse than we do." Melanesians delight in irony. "It's like this," said one of them afterwards, "a big boy is sitting on you and beating you, and you howl.—'What are you howling for?' he says. 'If I wasn't sitting on you, a bigger boy than I would be doing it, where's your gratitude?'" That was unfair, but the people feared they would be taxed more and more till they had nothing left.

I doubt if Melanesians ever had gaols. The nearest thing I ever heard of was on Mala. The first white man to walk across the island was Thomas Williams, a layman of our Mission. This was in 1901 when to undertake such a journey was really a mad thing to do. By all the rules he should have been killed when he walked from Fiu to Ataa. But he succeeded; and one of the things he saw in a central village was a very large cage made of bamboo in which an insane man was kept and fed.* You could call that a gaol. When the first real gaol was set up on San Cristoval it was not long before one of my Arosi friends went into it. When he came out I asked him what

* Arthur Hopkins also saw one of these.

he thought of this white man's custom. "Excellent," he said, "good food, good accommodation—but why did I get no pay?" The prisoners wore loin-cloths with broad arrows over them. These took the people's fancy. They were smuggled out, and in no time all the "best people" of Arosi were wearing them. There is no stigma in having been in gaol. Their view is that the man has done wrong. but he has paid for it, and is clear again. It seems in many ways a better view than ours. At all events gaols were something new. The Melanesian was always thinking "What next?" and "What will things be like at the end of it all?" He was puzzled, bewildered, and suspicious.

The Government official did not break things down as much as the missionary; and next to the missionary the one who brought about the greatest changes was the trader. If you asked any Melanesian, then or now, who was the most valuable member of the European group, he would say, the trader. By and large the European traders have been a great asset to the Solomon Islands. Workers on the plantations have been well treated, and their experience of this way of life has done them good; (of course on the other hand small villages have lost their most enterprising lads and those villages have stagnated). Many traders have been outstanding men, living in the Group for many years, unlike the Government officials, and giving an immense amount of help to the people among whom they lived. Many came and put all they had into plantations, only to see the price of copra go down till the plantation could not pay; and all their money and years of work were lost. It seemed to me that the Government view of the trader and planter was that he was a person to be tolerated, rather than to be encouraged and helped, especially when times were bad; and even often to be hindered and hampered by needless regulations. If Europeans had to leave the islands the Melanesians would have said, and would say now, let it be the trader last of all. He did not interfere with their customs, even if he laughed at their religion. He brought them goods they needed. He was fair and just. Their respect for the justice of white men, their belief that white men always keep their word and don't lie, is largely from their knowledge of the trader and planter. All the same these men have had a large share in the change that has come over the people, in some respects for the worse.

Fifty years ago you hardly ever saw anyone idle in a village. Everyone was making something, creating, and taking joy in it. It might be carving a spear or a club, or fashioning a native axe or adze or making a canoe, or inlaying a food bowl, or making tappa cloth or a mat, or a score of similar things. Then came a flood of foreign goods, better than they could make; axes and knives and calico and small boats and so on. They had to go on plantations or make copra to buy these things, and so their own industries and art ceased. Now you see young men in the villages sitting about idle all day. True, there are still their gardens to cultivate, but most of their creative work, in which they delighted, has come to an end. Only here and there, as in Tae Lagoon, where they are fisher folk and still work all day making and mending their nets, do you still see what you once saw in every village. In this way the trader has deeply affected the life of the people, even though he meant to help and not to harm them. He came of course to make money—why not? And like all our race he loved a spice of adventure in doing it.

Of course small misunderstandings between Europeans and Melanesians are inevitable, but there are many of them, and when added up they make things more difficult. Take two as examples. Europeans often say, quite falsely, that Melanesians have no sense of gratitude, and point to the fact that their languages have no word for "Thank you". There were a number of words in Arosi for this, not, we would say, quite decent; but they were only used to children or inferiors, never to equals or superiors. It is good manners for a Melanesian to receive a gift from an equal, still more from a superior, in silence.* To say anything is therefore to treat the giver as a child or inferior. They were surprised that Europeans insisted on being so treated but they are getting used to it now. Europeans simply said they had bad manners—"Not their fault, badly brought up". Or again, a Melanesian thinks it indecent for a man to put his arm round a lad's shoulder; their custom, which seems childish to us, is

---

* This is why, when the Duke of Edinburgh came to the Solomons the welcome was so quiet—it was all the deeper for that.

to take his hand in yours. However when they saw white men do what seemed to them improper, they simply said they had bad manners—"Not their fault, badly brought up". Both sides are now getting used to the bad manners of the other side.

To all these things add the many new diseases white men have brought in: dysentery, influenza, whooping cough, measles, polio, leprosy, and the rest. In my earlier years on San Cristoval an epidemic of dysentery used to sweep through the Group every year. After one such I went to visit a group of six bush villages, all small, but after that epidemic not one man, woman or child remained alive in any of them. The population was dying out rapidly because of the diseases introduced by the Europeans. In our medical work, which has increased so much in late years, we are not conferring a favour, we are paying a debt, we are trying to make amends.

No doubt the breaking down of their society, laws, customs and religion has helped to make the people feel both helpless and hopeless. Suppose a foreign nation had conquered our island, told us our religion was all childish superstition, made new laws continually without consulting us, judged us in their courts with no knowledge of our language, sold us their goods (better than ours) instead of letting us make our own, showed no interest in our language or customs and insisted on our learning theirs, treated us always as inferiors, always calling us "boys", brought in many strange diseases which were rapidly wiping us out; and suppose that *we knew we could do nothing about it*, because they were so infinitely stronger than we, might we not feel helpless and hopeless? The Melanesians did, and about thirty years ago I found the Arosi women refusing to have children, killing them by abortion, saying it was better so than that they should grow up in the white man's Solomons, and wishing they could send all white men packing; but they knew they never could. Thirty years later the Marching Rule men were saying: "Let us go back to our old way of life, our old customs and our old laws and religion, let us take an oath to drive out the British." Is it surprising? I must leave the other side of the picture to the next chapter.

CHAPTER SEVENTEEN

THE FUTURE

IN fifty years and more of my life in Melanesia the greatest change has been in the faces of the people. Many have felt that Heber's lines

> "Where every prospect pleases
> And only man is vile"

are a slander on the people of whom he wrote, and probably they were; but they would have been true of parts of heathenism in the Solomons. There you did see vile faces, many of them cruel, crafty and vicious; and now wherever you go you see, on the whole, faces that are kindly and have a dignity of their own. The Americans found it so in the war, to their great surprise; and the only reason for this is the adoption by the people of the Christian faith, the same faith by which the English live, even when they have outwardly rejected it. It is still in their subconscious.

Fifty years ago there was killing everywhere, killing for cannibal feasts, killing for money, killing for glory and revenge. Generally there was little or no bravery in it. Women and children in a garden were suddenly attacked and killed, a man fishing on the reef surrounded and speared, a village attacked just before dawn and everyone in it butchered. A stranger was killed as a matter of course. No one could land on another island without being killed. No one went twenty yards from his house without his weapons. Many have noticed in these days what heavy burdens of wood and water the women carry, and they have felt angry with the men for letting the women do it. Most newcomers write home about it and say that the women are beasts of burden. But fifty years ago when a woman went to gather wood and fetch water in her bamboo vessel, her husband could not help her to carry it for he had to walk beside her, with his weapons in his hands, alert for a killer. True, he need do so no longer; but the custom of the woman carrying the loads is ingrained from immemorial usage, and the woman is indignant if a man offers to do it. My own offers to take over the load of firewood under which some woman was bending were always laughingly or angrily rejected. No doubt the men should realise that times have changed. But the old days are not so long ago.

The people were very cruel. Many of the cruelties they practised cannot be printed, but the following are some of the less horrible. I have written of the child whose limbs, ears, and nose were lopped off to equalise the tally of killings. In Arosi the first-born baby was always killed. The father took it to the beach, dug a little hole, put the baby in with a large stone on top, and stamped on the stone. A friend of mine saw a man carried into a village, trussed to a pole like a pig, thrown down, and all the little children called to trample him to death; and another brought in thus, thrown on the fire alive, and eaten a few minutes later. The same cruelty was shown to animals. A living pig would be hung up and tortured to death with shouts of laughter. I was in a village when some hill people came down to visit my host, who had no food handy for them. He called his pet dog to him; the animal, though suspicious and growling a little, came wagging its tail. He swiftly wound a chain round its neck, strangled it, threw it on the fire, and in a few minutes he and his friends were eating his half-cooked pet. Cruelty amused them, so their faces grew vile. Nor was there truth in them. If a lie helped, a lie was always told. After all, is there any reason, if you are not a Christian, why you should not lie, if it helps you?

They lived in continual fear of black magic. If someone could get hold of anything belonging to you, your name or your possessions, or some part of you (hair, skin, and so on) he could make you fall sick and die. In Arosi there was the *here* (*vele* in Guadalcanar), a little bag with dead men's bones, which a man hidden by the path shook towards you and you died. Evil influences were everywhere, death was always near. Your expectation of life was a very short one. Treachery and cunning lay in wait for you on every side. The ordinary man or woman had no knowledge of the better religion of the priests. To the people the world was full of evil spirits, being the evil souls of the dead. Demon possession as in the New Testament—not the sort of thing our commentaries make it out to have been, but the real thing—was known to everyone. Is it surprising then that all that was good in them, and there is plenty of that in all men, turned eagerly to the teaching of Christ?

The old way of life was full of excitement. On Gela in those days people went on dancing parties from village to village, and it was a thrilling experience for the audience, because sometimes the dancing party had concealed weapons and in the middle of the dance fell on the watching people and massacred every one of them. You never knew what might happen when you went to see the dance! Men went into terrible rages and sweated blood. A Gela chief named Dikea went into one of these rages with his wife, for a very small matter, and beat her with a club till she was a bloody mess.

Life could be full of terror. But all the same it was full of colour, of rich ceremonial and of adventure; and to many it now seems drab and grey, just working for white men on plantations, or making copra or perhaps working in a mine; and as for excitement— nothing much. This is why many of the present generation, knowing nothing now of what life was really like fifty years ago, but hearing of the old customs, ceremonial, adventure and excitement, sometimes think wistfully of the old ways and wonder if European civilisation has been for them a blessing or a curse.

They know that with the coming of the Europeans they themselves have been rapidly dying out, and that this is still going on in some islands, that the population is static in others, and that it is increasing in only a few. Europeans know, from what has happened elsewhere in the Pacific, that more medical help and more preventive medicine, better food crops and more variety of food, can bring about a healthy and increasing race. The great work of an American doctor who conceived the idea of a medical school in Suva for Pacific Islanders, and brought it about, is bearing fruit. Mission hospitals are producing nurses. There is plenty of hope for the people; but they have not much faith yet, though it is growing, in their own future.

K

Europeans have been bringing unity to the people. Fifty years ago there was none. The people of one island, or even one district, knew little of any others, except that they were enemies. The great number of different languages kept them all apart from one another. But missionary, Government official and trader have all helped to bring about a growing unity. On the coconut plantations, year after year, some two thousand of the men from different islands came together, and got to know one another. They all spoke pidgin English. I am no believer in pidgin English as the future language of the whole people, it is too clumsy a medium of thought, but it has served a very useful purpose in thus drawing together people of different islands who had no common language.

Wishing to try everything and to know what it was like I was once allowed by a friendly trader to become for a time one of his plantation boys and live their life. We were up at 5.30 a.m. and after a cup of tea and a hard biscuit went out "brushing" the plantation, or making copra. We had a spell in the middle of the day and then worked till 5 p.m.—a nine-hour day. The evenings we spent in talk, boys from different islands all friendly together. It was a good life. The plantations have done as much as anything else to bring about the unity of the people, and break down the old hostilities and distrust of one another.

One Government for all, with one law for everyone, has also helped. The missionary has helped too, with one faith. This would have had the greatest effect of all if it had not been a divided Christianity which he brought them, making fresh divisions among them, divisions for which many of them see no reason, and which many of them think would cease but for the white missionaries among them. But like the plantations, the missionary schools have been a strong influence for bringing them all together, and getting rid of the suspicion and distrust they felt for one another. Not only have boys lived together in these schools for far longer periods than they ever spent on the plantations, but they have been able, because of this, to form lifelong friendships with boys from other islands than their own, and hundreds have gone as missionaries, often for life, to other parts of Melanesia. The great work the schools have done for unity has never been recognised. They ought to be helped and encouraged, for with a merely materialistic education the people— any people—will in the end wither and die. With the coming of girls' schools a new era is opening, because the women have a deeper influence in the village than the men. The white women who kept this aim always in view and worked their way towards it, have done more than anyone else in this generation for the Solomon Islanders. One of these, Sister Nellie Stead, a highly qualified nurse, especially in maternity work, well deserved the M.B.E. the Queen gave her.

What of the future? The Solomon Islanders are, and always have been, a race of small farmers. They have always been devoted to their land and taken pride in working their small farms. But they have worked them by primitive methods, the digging stick, not the plough. Men and women have divided the work, the men doing the heavy clearing, helping in the planting, and then leaving the gardens for the women to tend. They knew little or nothing of green manures, or cover crops, or rotation of crops, and so our schools have always been farms as well as schools, to give the boys better agricultural knowledge. Yet Melanesians are born farmers, and in their own ways very good ones, and know a great deal about soils and the way to plant tropical things, things that their rather scornful European critics don't know at all. The new self-supporting Church Association movement, though only at the beginning, has great future possibilities, not least because it originated with one of themselves, and has been worked out along Melanesian and original lines. The plan is for each island to have one or more of these church farms, leasing the land from their own people, paying their own people to run them and work them in their own way, but using better methods than in the past, and so spreading a knowledge of these better ways to every village on the island, and to every individual farm. They are growing new crops: rice, cocoa, and other things, hoping the villagers will follow suit, so that all will have more food and more variety than they had before; and that they will be able to sell their produce and so have more money than they once had for their needs. On their farms they hope to have cattle and poultry; to get hullers for the rice they grow, and some day tractors and such things to work their land. They will also, it is hoped, develop other industries. Once the people made pottery. Pamua, where I was at one time in charge of St. Michael's School, had been the headquarters of a pottery industry which died out before the white man came to the Solomons. In making our gardens at St. Michael's we used to dig up fragments of the pottery. My successor made a collection of shards which were sent to Dunedin museum, and the pottery was described in an article in the *Polynesian Journal*. Another friend of mine had a fine pot about two feet high, made at Pamua. The Islanders are also skilled in bamboo and rattan work; there are so many ways open to them with the materials they have at hand. Many have become good carpenters and engineers. They are skilful with their hands, but they feel that their skills at present are only being used for white men, not for themselves.

What of their art? They used to be great artists. A missionary visiting a San Cristoval village nearly a hundred years ago was amazed at the art in the great canoe house; beautifully carved figures of birds, fish and crocodiles; fine paintings, along both walls, of hunting scenes, fishing scenes and battles; excellent inlaid work. So it was once in many of the villages, but with the flood of European goods they lost interest in their own work. This art would have died out had it not been preserved to some extent in their churches. I remember going into a church in Ysabel. As you opened the door the whole interior seemed to flash silver: the altar, the lectern, even the pillars, were beautifully inlaid with mother-of-pearl. There were many carvings and a carved reredos. If you enter some of the Gela churches you find fine artistic work, and some really good paintings, mostly symbolic, by native artists, feeling their way to expressing themselves in a Melanesian manner. Or in Santa Cruz you find in a church their own Santa Cruzian decorative work in red, black and white. In all the islands you find it is the churches, and the churches almost alone, which have preserved their native art, which would otherwise have been lost long ago. There could well be a great revival. We have never done enough in this direction in our schools. Many of the people are true artists, but unencouraged and undeveloped. The revival of art among them ought to be along Melanesian lines. The same sort of thing could be said about their music, but I am not competent to write about it. We tend in all these things to teach them that only European art and European music are worth while. And finally there is drama. Their own religion was steeped in it. They love it. They are born actors in either comedy, where they far surpass us, or in tragedy. How little we have done to develop these things! We have destroyed so much. We have neglected a whole side of their nature. Can we wonder if life seems to them now more drab and grey than it once was, and that they look back wistfully to past glories?

However, in one mission school at least, this native love of drama has been encouraged. Eleven years ago I paid a visit to All Hallows, Pawa, of which I had been Headmaster more than twenty years earlier. While I was there the Headmaster happened to find out that the next day was my seventieth birthday and he decided to give the boys a holiday in my honour. Next morning after the daily Eucharist we had an excellent breakfast (he is one of the best cooks in the Mission), then he said to me, "Now, go and sit on that chair at the top of the steps on the verandah and see what happens!" I felt rather nervous. I knew the tradition of the school was to throw the Headmaster into the sea on his birthday—the junior masters, I fancy, only into the swamp—and I wondered nervously what might be in store for a former Headmaster. All was silent, no one was about, and the minutes passed slowly. Then suddenly from some bushes rushed an old man, with a white beard, and a sharp scythe in his hands. He said he was Father Time and had come to cut me down because I had reached three score years and ten. He came at me too as if he meant to do it! At the last moment out rushed Youth, dressed in gold and with garlands of flowers about him. He threw himself in Father Time's path, calling out to him that I was a *young* old man and must not die, then he lifted his sword and fought with Father Time, and in spite of his scythe laid him low in the dust. (I was sorry for Father Time; it was very hot, he lay on sharp gravel, and there he had to lie dead for some time). Youth took my hand and led me to his band of garlanded attendants, who set me in the midst of them and sang a magic song and danced round me so that my days might be long. Then four big fellows with blackened faces, who told me they were cannibals, dashed up. I did not mind cannibals, I was used to them. They set me in a chair and lifted me high and bore me to the other end of the hill on which the school stands and there all the school were assembled for a feast—yams, taro, bananas, pork, beef, and so on. "Some refreshments!" said the Headmaster, and though it was just after breakfast we sat down to the feast.

"Now," said the Headmaster, "we are going down to the cricket ground and you are going to captain the masters against the boys." I had played very little cricket since I was sixty, but this Headmaster had a way with him. We had to go. I won the toss and put our side in, but the boys were in form and the first six masters were soon out for five runs, though our No. 1 was holding up his wicket well. I felt it was up to me. No. 1 and I made fifty-one—that is to say, I blocked in a dignified way and poked an occasional single, while my partner hit out and made the runs. We were all out for sixty, but the boys were all out for twenty-six. They pulled nearly every ball, so I put almost all our fieldsmen on the on side and got them caught, a very convenient arrangement. Besides we had the hospital nurse, playing as one of the masters, and fielding at longstop. When the ball passed the wicket-keeper she just curtsied, and they got no byes.

"Now," said the Headmaster, "for some refreshments!"

So we went to the shore and there had another feast of yams, taro, bananas, pork and beef. Most enjoyable.

"Now," said the Headmaster, "we are going back to the playing fields for some football matches." We had two or three. One gets confused on these days at Pawa. Did I play or referee? They were very good hard games.

"Now," said the Headmaster, "for some refreshments!" This time light ones: sandwiches, cake, tea.

"Now," said the Headmaster, "the boys are going to do some dances for you." Very good they were, full of colour and the boys danced with spirit.

"Now," said the Headmaster, "we are going up the hill for your birthday dinner." It was evening by that time. It was a good dinner: soup, roast beef and yorkshire pudding, vegetables, fruit salad and coffee.

After Evensong the Headmaster said, "Now the boys are putting on some plays for you." It was Thomas à Becket. He was in scarlet and very fat. He looked to me a very proud prelate and I was glad the barons killed him. (When I go to Pawa the boys always seem to be killing one of the saints; another time it was Polycarp. They burnt him, actually tied him to a stake with faggots round him, and lit the fire too, with copies of the Church Times, showing how old that paper is, and then just as the fire was going well, and Polycarp looking anxious, the curtain unfortunately came down.) After Thomas à Becket came Cinderella, the Headmaster enjoying himself hugely as the prince. After the plays there was a sing-song, the Headmaster leading the boys in "Polly wolly doodle all the day"!

After that (it was midnight) the Headmaster said, "Now for some refreshments!" So we went over to his house, just beer and a smoke this time, and then he called it a day.

This sort of thing is what we want more of in Melanesia! The Headmaster was given the M.B.E. for his "educational work", and very sound it was. More life, and more abounding life, is what the Melanesians need. We have taken away the exciting and adventurous in their life, and set them to making copra. If they want excitement there is ping-pong in a boys' club. They are bored.

A leading member of the Mission tells me he thinks, because some of our islands in the Solomons are half empty, we should invite the Japanese or others in crowded countries to come and populate them.

These islands, no doubt, are half empty; and it is we who have made them so, by destroying their old life and by bringing in so many new forms of disease. It seems rather bad taste on the part of the murderer to offer a friend the victim's possessions.

The case is rather similar in Fiji, where the Indian population, invited into Fiji by the British, seems likely in time to displace altogether the Fijians. Australia is half empty but insists on only white immigrants. New Zealand is much the same. It is Nathan's story to David over again. The Rich Man, the British Empire, will not offer to its friends in Asia any of its many wide and empty lands, but they may willingly have the Poor Man's lamb, all he has, the small islands of the Fijians or the Solomon Islanders. The weak to the wall is the way of the world!

The argument goes on: are not the Solomon Islanders a race of inferior mental capacity, not worth preserving? I never quite know what to say to that, because the mental capacity of my Melanesian friends is much the same as my own. It seems humiliating to answer yes, and conceited to say no.

Given medical and agricultural help the race can be saved; but not by big schemes, nor by spending a lot of money. They can work out their own salvation and it is better that they should. It might be good for the islands to come under Australia or New Zealand because these countries are nearer than Britain and have a vital interest in the future of the islands. Australia has its hands full in the great island of New Guinea, so New Zealand might be better; and it has a good record in Samoa and with its own Maoris. It can help most by sending teachers to train and inspire many of the two thousand boys in our Solomon Island boarding schools, so that the people may have good Christian leaders when they eventually achieve self-government.

Some day there may be a Federation of the island groups: Samoa, Tonga, Fiji, the New Hebrides and the Solomons, with Fiji at the head; and possibly including New Caledonia and New Britain, one in the south and one in the north;* but meanwhile, and for many years yet, each of these groups must develop independently and learn self-government.

It has suddenly been discovered by the whole world that "colonialism" is a wicked thing. But British colonialism, so widely criticised today, has been a good thing for the Solomon Islanders. To begin with they needed protection from exploitation when they could not protect themselves. As the years went on a British government gave

* This would seem to involve the right of a citizen of each group to settle in any other, which the groups might not be willing to concede.

them law and order and had a very large share in welding them into one people. But it could do them harm by trying to do too much for them, and trying to make them as much as possible British, instead of helping them to work out their own salvation. The Solomon Islanders are worth saving.

MELANESIA AND THE MELANESIANS

WHERE is Melanesia, and who are the Melanesians?

Indonesia is known to be an early name, and its islands, such as Java, Sumatra, Borneo and the Phillipines were well known in early times; but the other groups of Pacific islands were named much later. In 1833, the navigator d'Urville named all the groups in the middle of the Pacific—Samoa, Tonga, Hawaii and many others—Polynesia, "the many islands". Sailing west from Tonga he came to Fiji and was surprised to find people quite different from the Polynesians he knew. He tells us they were much darker, blue-black in appearance, with hairy bodies, and he called the islands Melanesia, "the black islands"—though in fact most of the inhabitants are chocolate-coloured, some fairer, some darker.

The name Melanesia was given to all the groups of islands from Fiji to the south-east coast of New Guinea, where the people were like the Fijians* and where most of them spoke languages akin to Fijian, quite different from Polynesian languages. The islands which make up Melanesia are: Fiji itself; New Caledonia; the New Hebrides; two groups of small islands, the Banks and Torres Islands; Santa Cruz and the Reef Islands; the Solomons; New Britain and New Ireland, a long chain of islands running roughly north-west from Fiji. All the small groups to the north of Melanesia (the Gilbert and Ellice Islands, the Carolines and others), d'Urville named Micronesia.

The name does not tell us much about the people themselves. We can learn more from their languages. The languages of Indonesia, Polynesia and Melanesia all belong to one great family of languages called Austronesian, the original speakers of which probably came from south-east Asia and migrated in very early times to Indonesia.

* It is surprising how often the Fijians are wrongly called Polynesians.

The rest that follows is my own reading of the story from a study of the languages, and of course it may not be the right one.

Very long ago these Austronesians, living at that time in Indonesia, migrated in large numbers into Melanesia, coming down from the north to the central Solomon Islands. Here they found negrito people, small and dark, whom they conquered, moving from the central Solomons along the line of the trade winds, south-east through the eastern Solomons, the Torres and Banks Islands and the northern New Hebrides to Fiji, which was as far as they got. This is the area where the Melanesian languages are truly Austronesian. They missed the Santa Cruz group and Reef Islands to the north, and to a large extent the southern New Hebrides and New Caledonia, though their influence was felt there, as it was also to the west of the central Solomons right up to and including the south-east coast of New Guinea.

In this area, from Ysabel in the Solomons to Fiji, they settled in large numbers, becoming one people with the negritoes whom they found there, imposing their language, although adding words to it from the negrito languages; and for a time imposing a general peace. There is a tradition of this general peace, long before the Spaniard Mendana's discovery of them in 1565, when there was general trading among the island peoples.

The Austronesians who were left in Indonesia most likely received a migration from another people, probably from India, with whom they became one, keeping their own language but having it added to and modified by the newcomers. Then after a time there was another great migration, this time into Polynesia, then probably uninhabited. Gradually they took possession of all the Polynesian groups; a few found their way south into Melanesia.

Those who still remained in Indonesia were in time deeply influenced by other peoples coming in, and so we come to the modern Indonesians. But the original Austronesian language, modified in different ways by different peoples, has persisted as the basis of their speech among all the peoples of the Pacific, in the three great groups of Indonesia, Polynesia, and Melanesia. It is one of the great ancient languages of the world.

The Melanesian form of Austronesian is, I think, the oldest, older than that of Indonesia and Polynesia.* having somewhat the same relation to these as Sanskrit has to European languages. It is in Melanesia that you find the earliest forms of Austronesian grammar and words, and without a knowledge of the Melanesian grammar and vocabulary the history of Indonesian and Polynesian languages cannot be followed or understood. But both these languages have had new elements added to them after the Austronesians came to Melanesia, and the Austronesian of Melanesia has itself been modified by the languages of the people they found there. That is how I read the story.

Coming to the Melanesians I know best, that is to say those in the islands from Ysabel in the Solomons to Fiji, you find several forms of language. The Austronesian languages are the main ones, spoken by most of the people, but there are also here and there the older negrito languages, probably pre-Austronesian, chiefly on small islands. These are completely different from the Austronesian languages. When you pass from, say, the language of Gela in the Solomons to that of Laumbe (Russell Islands) or even to that of Savo, you come to languages of a quite different type, which have sometimes been called Papuan. As you go west you come to similar languages, or again as you go north-east to Santa Cruz and some of the Reef Islands, such as Nifilole or Tuo, or to Utupua and Vanikolo, or farther south-east to the southern New Hebrides. These languages, so different each from the other, may not all belong to one family, but they are all quite different from Austronesian.

Also in Melanesia you find some Polynesian languages spoken on small outlying islands: Tikopia, Anuda, Sikaiana, Munggava, Munggiki (Rennell and Bellona), Lord Howe (Liuniua), Nukumanu and some of the Reef Islands (Matema, Nukapu, Pileni). Sir Peter Buck thought them a backwash from Polynesia, but the evidence is against this. The language of Rennell for instance is much nearer to the Maori of New Zealand than to Samoan or Tongan. I think myself that when the early Polynesians passed through Micronesia on their way to Polynesia, some of them found their way down south

* Some would not agree with me about this.

to these islands, while the rest of them went on east. Later, I think much later, Polynesians did come from central Polynesia and found their way to these islands, already occupied by much older bands of Polynesians belonging to the time of the great migration into Polynesia.

From the way in which the pre-Austronesian languages differ so much from each other, it seems when the Austronesians came down from the north they may have found several hundred different languages spoken in the Solomons, and so were forced to make their own language a lingua franca, just as the Europeans coming now and finding less than a hundred languages spoken in the group still find them too many, and want to teach everyone English.

But if Austronesian was a lingua franca why should there be so many varieties of it now, so that men like S. H. Ray have spoken of one hundred languages in the Solomons? In the first place one must subtract the negrito and Polynesian languages spoken in the Solomons from that number, leaving perhaps eighty. In the second place, many of these are dialects rather than languages; thus making only three or four languages for Mala instead of the usual ten or twelve. In fact ten or twelve is about the right number of distinct languages in the group. Even so it is remarkable that there are so many, and so many dialects in addition. There may have been several waves of Austronesian invaders. Moreover, after the ancient peace there followed many hundred years of fighting and the consequent isolation of each island, or even of several districts in one island, each isolated from the next, and all the time gradual language changes were going on. We have, however, records of the languages as they were a hundred years ago, and in that time there has been little or no change. In Verguet's list of Arosi words collected in the last century there is only one word different now, the word for a ship; *haka* now, instead of *waka* then. So the great differences in the dialects and languages must have come about over a very long period of time. In different islands the Austronesians may have met with different negrito languages, and so adopted different words; but the negrito element in these languages is so small that this cannot be of much importance. Now, of course, English words are pouring into their languages, and not only names of things they did not have before. The old Gela word for "stale" was *madiri*. Now that has dropped out and they use the word phonetically written *tuleti*, which is really the English "too late". There are many such; though it is only their vocabularies, not their grammars, that have been affected by English speakers.

The people of San Cristoval speak of the earliest immigrants as the people of *Tawa*. There is no "J" or "V" in their language so that Java would be called Tawa by them. It may be they came from there. There are three forms of one original word which are now the names of islands in the Solomons, Mala, Nggela, and Gera, the last being the old native name for a large part, at least, of the island Guadalcanar, and the other two still in use as the names of islands. These three forms are etymologically the same from an original root *Kala*, but I do not know of a Kala in Indonesia.

It has been impossible in a few pages to give the evidence for this sketch of Melanesian history. Others will have different views; I have merely given the view which seems to myself the most likely according to the linguistic evidence.